you & your wedding

The WEDDING PLANNER

you & your wedding

The WEDDING PLANNER

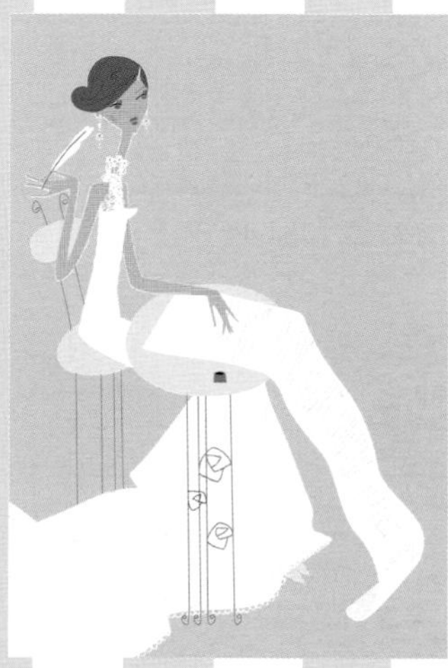

Carole Hamilton
illustrations by Max Savva

foulsham
LONDON • NEW YORK • TORONTO • SYDNEY

foulsham
The Publishing House
Bennetts Close
Cippenham
Slough
Berkshire SL1 5AP
England

For Nick and George

Foulsham books can be found in all good bookshops and direct from www.foulsham.com

ISBN: 978-0-572-03345-3

A CIP record for this book is available from the British Library

Other books in this series:
The Groom's Guide (978-0-572-03265-4)
The Bride's Book (978-0-572-03316-3)
The Best Man's Book (978-0-572-03366-8)
Your Wedding Vows, Words and Music (978-0-572-03374-3)

While every effort has been made to ensure the accuracy of all the information contained within this book, neither the author nor the publisher can be liable for any errors. In particular, since laws change from time to time, it is vital that each individual checks relevant legal details for themselves.

Every effort has been made to contact copyright holders of the extracts included in this book. Where it has not been possible to trace any copyright holder, despite our best endeavours, we would ask that anyone claiming such copyright should contact the publisher with full details, and if an author's copyright has been inadvertently infringed sincere apologies are tendered.

Printed in Dubai

Design: Matthew Inman (www.spinning-top.com)

Contents

It all starts here

... the long road to the aisle has many ups and downs and I hope The Wedding Planner will make that journey just a little simpler for you

Until recently I was the editor of *You & Your Wedding* magazine and, after 13 years in the job and the privilege and experience of helping thousands of girls to plan and enjoy their weddings, I've packed this book with all my insider knowledge to help you plan your special day. Having been asked for advice on everything from sorting out seating plans to ordering flowers, selecting a good photographer to choosing the perfect dress, I know just about everything there is to know about the highs and lows of what it takes to plan any kind of wedding.

Planning even a small wedding takes some pretty nifty managing to bring it all together on time, on budget and looking amazing, which is why I think you'll find *The Wedding Planner* so helpful. It takes you through every stage of planning your wedding, whatever the style and whatever the budget. I've taken a no-frills approach so all you get are the facts plus lots of handy checklists to accompany each stage of the planning process.

As you progress through your engagement you'll find that planning your big day is all a bit of a juggling act. There are so many decisions to make that keeping track of what you've already done and what still needs to be done can become a nightmare. To help you keep bang up-to-date with everything on your 'to do' list, each section of *The Wedding Planner* has a selection of wedding worksheets that I think you'll find invaluable. There's also plenty of room to jot down contact numbers and e-mail addresses as well as space to make your own notes.

I can't promise you a completely smooth route from engagement to the aisle but I do hope *The Wedding Planner* will make your journey a lot less stressful. Enjoy it!

Carole Hamilton

For more help with every aspect of planning your wedding check out www.youandyourwedding.co.uk. It's packed with information and there's a buzzing chatroom with other brides-to-be all sharing their experiences of this wonderful journey.

To do list

First Things First

Getting married is a hugely exciting time, full of love, laughter and probably a few tears – and it all starts here with those all-important decisions that will make your wedding day truly unique.

The key questions

Q What is your dream? **Sit down with your fiancé and each make a list of everything that's important to you both. Split the list into essentials (venue, dress, flowers and so on) and optionals (limo, chocolate fountain, string quartet) to give you both a clear picture of your dream day. Compare your lists and agree to compromise where necessary.**

Q What is your overall style? **Will you be having a religious or a civil ceremony? How many guests do you want to invite? Will it be a formal or more casual reception? Would a wedding abroad work for you?**

Q What size is your wedding budget? **How are you going to pay for the wedding? Will parents be contributing? How much can you save up during your engagement? Will you need to think about taking out a loan to pay for some of the expenses?**

Q Do you have a date in mind? **Do you want a short or a long engagement? Are there any major family occasions coming up that will cause scheduling problems? Is the time of year important?**

The answers to these questions will help you to put together a clearer vision of what will be included in your perfect day and, of course, whether you can afford to pay for your dream wedding.

Do you share the same ideas?

When it comes to the wedding vision, try putting the 10 factors listed below in order of importance (1 for highest priority, 10 for lowest) and get your fiancé to do the same. It will quickly reveal whether you have the same ideas about what makes the ideal wedding.

- a fabulous dress/designer suit
- a spectacular venue
- the ceremony
- having as many guests as possible
- an amazing honeymoon
- serving a gourmet meal and fine wines
- filling the venues with flowers
- wow-factor entertainment (such as fireworks)
- unusual transport (a horse and carriage, for example)
- an open bar all evening

Hopefully that wasn't too painful and, once you have some ideas about the when, where and how much surrounding your big day, you can involve parents and other close friends and relatives in your decisions.

Spreading the good news

Good news is always best delivered in person and both of you should tell each set of parents together. Tell other family members and friends next, if possible letting everyone know the wedding date so they can pencil it into their diaries.

Be prepared to answer questions as word spreads – everyone loves a wedding and will be full of advice on everything from the venue to colour schemes. Be polite, say you'll keep their ideas in mind and remember to keep smiling.

If you are planning your wedding for the traditionally busy 'wedding season' from June to September, when friends may be invited to other weddings or have their own holiday plans, sending out 'save the date' cards early on is a good idea.

You may also like to share your happy news with the wider world by putting an announcement in your local and/or a national newspaper. Something simply worded like this:

Mr and Mrs John Brown of Sevenoaks
are delighted to announce the engagement of their daughter Amy
to Barry Smith of Guildford, Surrey
A September 2008 wedding is being planned

A wedding announcement used to be followed by an engagement party with lots of lovely presents for the happy couple's new home. These days, because many couples already live together, formal engagement parties are becoming less popular. But if you want to throw a party – and why not? – you can always make it clear on the invitations that your friends' company is enough and you don't expect armfuls of gifts.

Now is also the time to start thinking about the people you want to play a key part in your wedding plans, from your mother and your best friend to the best man and ushers.

What is your wedding style?

The key questions

Q Do you want a traditional wedding? **This is the most popular – and usually most expensive – style of wedding, with a religious or civil ceremony followed by a drinks reception, a seated meal in the late afternoon or early evening, and then a party with dancing to live music or with a DJ.**

First Things First
Your Wedding Ceremony
Your Suppliers
Your Reception
Dressed to Thrill
Your Wedding Gifts
Your Honeymoon
One Week and Counting

Q Is informal more your style? **A more casual reception usually follows a civil ceremony and involves a buffet-style reception or cocktail party in the afternoon with guests departing in the late afternoon. It's ideal if you don't like a lot of fuss and it can be very cost effective if you are on a tight budget.**

Q What about the wedding weekend? **This is an increasingly popular option if you want to splash out and entertain a smaller number of guests over a weekend. It usually involves arriving at a venue on Friday, the wedding taking place during the day on Saturday followed by a formal reception, then everyone meeting up again on Sunday for breakfast before leaving for home.**

Having decided on the overall style of the wedding day, the ceremony and how you are going to feed and entertain your guests, you need to take a moment to think about the time of year you are marrying. The season will be your guide as you plan the colour scheme and decorative touches that will bring individual flair to the whole day.

Style through the seasons

Choosing a theme of some kind is a great way to co-ordinate your wedding and will always add a touch of style. It doesn't have to be anything fancy; seasonal colour is the simplest option and will tie your whole day together, so it works beautifully.

If you choose a spring wedding, you can make the most of the lighter evenings by choosing a venue with lots of windows. The weather is pretty changeable so you are likely to be celebrating indoors. Suitable seasonal colour themes might be bright and sunny white or perhaps a subdued palette of soft pinks, lilac and moss greens.

When you think of summer sunshine, you think of white or pastels, which always look cool on a sunny day. Choose fabrics such as organza or voile that flutter in the breeze, and put up oversize white umbrellas to create welcome shade for your guests. Since you can't guarantee the weather, think very carefully before you choose to eat outside; a conservatory with doors you can open or a marquee with open sides are both solutions that would let in the evening air but provide cover at the same time. Decorate any outside areas with strings of fairy lights or put lanterns in the trees to keep the party going as darkness descends.

All the amazing autumnal colours can make a stunning input into your colour scheme. You don't have to go too 'harvest festival' with the whole look – a glorious rich aubergine, silky russet and every shade of gold work equally well at this time of the year. The evenings will be drawing in so, if your venue allows it, make candlelight a big part of your decoration. Tea lights can be used in many different ways and are an inexpensive (and safe) way to add a romantic glow to any room.

Rich red, greens and gold make a perfect winter choice or, for a more contemporary look, why not go for ice white? If your wedding is near Christmas, the venue may well already be decked out with Christmas trees and decorations so you'll be half-way there. Christmas decorations, bought in bulk, are wonderfully versatile and can be heaped into inexpensive glass containers for decoration or hung from silver-sprayed twigs. The days will be short so candlelight and fairy lights will be much more atmospheric than overhead lighting.

WEDDING WORKSHEET

Your wedding priorities

This will help to give you a clearer picture of the most important elements for your big day.

	Very important	Important	Not important
Before the day			
Engagement announcement			
Engagement party			
Engagement ring			
Wedding dress			
Groom's suit			
Prenuptial agreement			
Pre-marriage counselling			
Invitations			
Professional hair and make-up			
Hen party			
Stag party			
Rehearsal dinner			
Other			
Ceremony			
Small (family only)			
Big (everyone you know)			
Religious			
Civil			
Same location as ceremony			
Live music			
Readings			
Best man			
Chief bridesmaid			
Other bridesmaids			
Flower girl			
Page boy			

	Very important	Important	Not important
Wedding rings			
Wedding transport			
Venue decoration			
Bouquet			
Photography			
Video			
Reception			
Receiving line			
Table plan			
Cocktail welcome			
Canapés			
Sit-down meal			
Buffet			
Favours			
Open bar			
Top table			
Toastmaster			
Speeches			
Toasts			
Wedding cake			
Cake-cutting ceremony			
Live music			
DJ			
Entertainment			
Gifts for maids/mums/best man			
Evening guests			
First dance			
Fireworks			
Grand exit			
First night hotel			
Honeymoon			

Your budget

The key questions

Q Who is paying? **It used to be that the bride's father pretty much paid for everything. These days it's far more likely to be a family affair with the bride, groom and both sets of parents chipping in to create one wedding fund.**

Q Will you need to compromise your ideas? **Taking a cheque from either set of parents is great. Just be sure they don't think this means they have a much bigger say in your wedding plans than you want. It's hard to say you want workmates rather than relatives on the guest list if it's your parent's cash you are spending.**

Q Is going it alone an option? **It's becomingly increasingly common for couples to pay for their own wedding, using their own money – and it's the only way to ensure complete freedom of choice. If the cash isn't readily available, seek advice about saving and cost-effective borrowing.**

Budget planning

Lots of couples do pay for their own wedding and it's perfectly possible to have an amazing wedding on just about any budget. You simply need to start organising from the word go.

Start saving

Saving 10–20 per cent of every pay packet during your engagement should be your aim. Try a few cost-cutting measures every month like taking a packed lunch to work, staying in with friends rather than eating out, and delaying major purchases or expensive outings until after the wedding.

A wedding account

Whether or not you are receiving parental contributions, a separate wedding account is a good idea since it will make tracking what comes in, what goes out and what's left to play with much simpler. Agree at the outset how much you will each contribute to the fund, taking into account your differing salaries and any other debts you may have.

Get financial advice

If you need help with the wedding fund and are thinking about a loan, get advice on the best way of borrowing. A small loan may be worthwhile, providing you can pay it back without being in debt for years to come – not even your wedding is worth that! And forget putting wedding expenses on a credit card; it's expensive and is usually a recipe for financial misery.

Do it yourself

Think carefully about whether you can do some things yourself rather than employing others to do them: check out eBay (www.ebay.co.uk) for wedding bargains – new and 'once-loved'; look out for sample sales at your local wedding dress shop; get on to your PC and design your own invitations, thank-you cards or seating plan.

How will you spend the cash?

Once you have a good idea of your budget, you'll need to split the pot between the various parts of the wedding. Here we are using the national average of around £20,000* but the same formula works on any budget.

The average wedding budget*

Reception, including food and drink	40%	£ 8,000
Venue/ceremony/musicians	15%	£ 3,000
Outfits	10%	£ 2,000
Flowers/entertainment/transport	10%	£ 2,000
Photography/video	7%	£ 1,250
Stationery	3%	£ 750
Honeymoon	10%	£ 2,000
Unexpected extras	5%	£ 1,000
Total budget	**100%**	**£20,000**

* *You & Your Wedding* Readership Survey 2006

Scary isn't it? What seemed like a decent budget when you started doesn't look very much once you've split it up. But don't get disheartened; there are lots of ways to make your money go a long way and, remember, great weddings are not about how much you spend!

Stretching the budget

The reception takes the biggest slice of the budget and, since the amount you spend is directly in line with how many guests you invite, take a long, hard look at the proposed guest list. Every guest you invite is going to cost you money and you have to ask yourself if each one really needs to be invited. Now look at the rest of the day to see where you can cut costs without your guests noticing!

- Aim for a shorter day – the longer your guests are with you, the more you have to pay to feed, water and entertain them.
- A weekday wedding will mean better deals from many suppliers since you are avoiding popular (and expensive) weekends.
- Have a select dinner and invite most guests to an evening-only party.
- Think about hiring rather than buying your wedding outfits.
- Forget the formal sit-down dinner and have a stylish cocktail and canapés party instead. Serve interesting finger food, cocktails and lots of champagne and everyone will think you are being trendy, not cheap!
- Choose the less-is-more theory when it comes to flowers and decorations. One or two large, eye-catching arrangements are often more impressive than individual table centrepieces.
- Find out if there's another wedding at your ceremony venue on the same day and see if you can split the flower budget.
- Serve sparkling wine rather than champagne and check out the venue's house wines, which are usually very good.
- Give live music a miss. Use the venue's sound system and play compilation CDs of your favourite music.
- Have a pay bar once the formal meal is over.

The wedding budget

The only way to keep an accurate grip on what you've spent and what you still have to buy.

	Estimate	Actual	Deposit paid	Balance due
Ceremony				
Licence fee	£	£	£	£
Location fee	£	£	£	£
Officiant's fee	£	£	£	£
Music	£	£	£	£
Wedding outfits				
Bride's wedding ring	£	£	£	£
Groom's wedding ring	£	£	£	£
Bride's dress	£	£	£	£
Headdress	£	£	£	£
Veil	£	£	£	£
Accessories	£	£	£	£
Shoes	£	£	£	£
Lingerie	£	£	£	£
Hair	£	£	£	£
Make-up	£	£	£	£
Groom's outfit	£	£	£	£
Accessories	£	£	£	£
Bridesmaids' dresses	£	£	£	£
Accessories	£	£	£	£
Reception				
Venue fee	£	£	£	£
Items to hire (linens etc.)	£	£	£	£
Canapés	£	£	£	£
Meal (per head x no. of guests)	£	£	£	£
Waiting staff	£	£	£	£

	Estimate	Actual	Deposit paid	Balance due
Wine	£	£	£	£
Champagne	£	£	£	£
Soft drinks	£	£	£	£
Evening bar	£	£	£	£
Cake	£	£	£	£
Favours	£	£	£	£
Flowers/decorations				
Ceremony decorations	£	£	£	£
Bride's bouquet	£	£	£	£
Bridesmaids' bouquets	£	£	£	£
Buttonholes	£	£	£	£
Corsages	£	£	£	£
Centrepieces	£	£	£	£
Cake table flowers	£	£	£	£
Reception venue flowers	£	£	£	£
Music/entertainment				
Ceremony musicians	£	£	£	£
Reception musicians	£	£	£	£
Evening band/DJ	£	£	£	£
Other entertainment	£	£	£	£
Photography/video				
Photographer's fee	£	£	£	£
Videographer's fee	£	£	£	£
Extra prints	£	£	£	£
Copies of video	£	£	£	£
Disposable cameras	£	£	£	£

	Estimate	Actual	Deposit paid	Balance due
Stationery				
Save the date cards	£	£	£	£
Invitations	£	£	£	£
RSVP cards	£	£	£	£
Stamps	£	£	£	£
Order of service	£	£	£	£
Seating plan	£	£	£	£
Place cards	£	£	£	£
Menus	£	£	£	£
Thank-you cards	£	£	£	£
Transport				
Bride's car	£	£	£	£
Maids'/bride's mum's car	£	£	£	£
Groom's self-drive car	£	£	£	£
Shuttle bus	£	£	£	£
Parking fees	£	£	£	£
Miscellaneous				
Wedding planner	£	£	£	£
Wedding insurance	£	£	£	£
First night hotel room	£	£	£	£
Attendants' gifts	£	£	£	£
Gifts for mothers	£	£	£	£
Honeymoon	£	£	£	£
Tips	£	£	£	£
Grand total	£			
Other				
Allow 5–10% of the total budget for unexpected extras.				

When do you want to marry?

The key questions

Q How long do you need? This is the key to everything – the amount of time you need to plan (and pay) for your big day! The average engagement in the UK is around 17 months but you can do it a lot quicker or take longer. This one is really up to you.

Q Is there a special day for you? The anniversary of when you met or the date of one set of parents' wedding anniversary are both nice ideas. Some couples fancy combining a major family celebration such as a birthday, Easter or Christmas with their wedding. And, for the ultimate in romance, you could always try Valentine's Day. Just remember, the competition for suppliers around popular dates will be fierce – and prices will probably reflect this popularity as well.

Q Does the time of year matter? If your dream day involves sunshine and sipping champagne on the lawn, then a summer wedding is for you: if you can be more flexible about the season then you could save money. It's all about supply and demand and suppliers are much more likely to be open to price negotiations in the 'low season' and if you can be flexible about having a weekday wedding.

Q What's available? Lots of venues, suppliers and even the registrar are booked up to a year in advance, so you'll have to make a few phone calls to check availability before setting your heart on one particular date. This is especially important when it comes to the registrar; you need to be sure they are free to marry you before you make any commitment to booking a venue.

Setting the wedding date

You'll need to narrow down your options and think about various – perhaps competing – demands.

	Plus points	Minus points
Venue		
Time offered		
Special days		
Season		
Price		

The venue shortlist

Use this worksheet for tracking contacts and keeping notes after each of the prospective venues you visit.

Venue name

Contact name

Telephone number

E-mail address

Website

Your notes

Venue name

Contact name

Telephone number

E-mail address

Website

Your notes

Venue name

Contact name

Telephone number

E-mail address

Website

Your notes

Venue name

Contact name

Telephone number

E-mail address

Website

Your notes

Venue name

Contact name

Telephone number

E-mail address

Website

Your notes

Venue name

Contact name

Telephone number

E-mail address

Website

Your notes

Venue name

Contact name

Telephone number

E-mail address

Website

Your notes

First Things First
Your Wedding Ceremony
Your Suppliers
Yourr Reception
Dressed to Thrill
Your Wedding Gifts
Your Honeymoon
One Week and Counting

General planning

The key questions

Q What type of wedding do you want? Every wedding takes a lot of planning but a large, elaborate celebration can be very time consuming and stressful, so you need to be prepared. When you think about what makes up your perfect day, also factor in what it's going to take to organise such an event. It may be worth thinking about using a wedding planner, leaving you time to think about the finer details.

Q How much time do you have? You need to ask yourself not only how much planning time you think you'll have, but also how much time you actually want to spend on your wedding. It's not everyone's idea of fun to spend every weekend devoted to wedding planning. If you know that your work, hobbies and social life take up a large proportion of your time, then perhaps you should be thinking of a smaller celebration. Planning a wedding is supposed to be fun, not a chore!

Q How much help will you get? Accept early on that you're not superwoman and that you'll need help and support from your fiancé, your family and friends if the wedding is to come together without you having a nervous breakdown. Make lists of tasks that can be delegated and agree on times for regular update meetings so you still feel that everything is under your ultimate control.

Q Is the budget big or small? The size of your budget will impact on how much time and effort you'll have to put into the planning process. The more you spend, the more experts you can pay to help you! And while this is great for your stress levels, just make sure that you are still making all the key decisions – it's still your wedding after all!

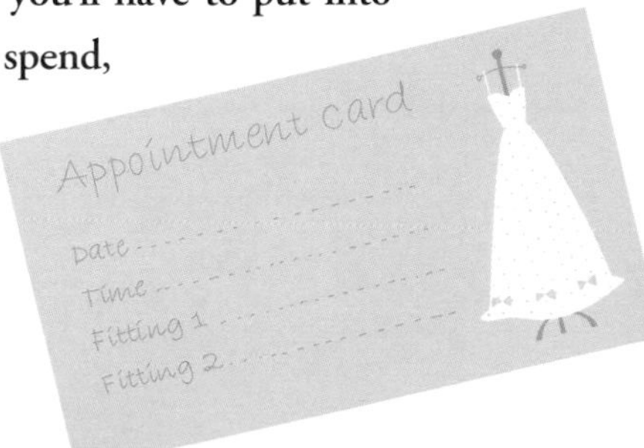

The planning checklist

Planning a wedding takes a lot of work. Here's what needs to be done and when.

As soon as possible

- ❑ Tell relatives and close friends your happy news
- ❑ Put an announcement in the local paper
- ❑ Arrange the first meeting with the minister or registrar
- ❑ For a civil ceremony, book the registrar and register office/civil venue
- ❑ Set the budget
- ❑ Ask parents if they would like to contribute
- ❑ Choose your best man, bridesmaids and other attendants
- ❑ Decide on the number of guests and draw up a potential list to discuss
- ❑ Visit possible venues
- ❑ Post 'save the date' cards, if required
- ❑ Discuss menus with possible caterers and get estimates for the food and drink
- ❑ Make all reception bookings
- ❑ Start looking for your wedding dress and attendants' outfits
- ❑ Book your photographer and videographer
- ❑ Arrange wedding insurance

Three months before

- ❑ Arrange a second meeting with your minister to discuss the ceremony and agree a date for publication of the banns. If the ceremony is to be in a church other than the Church or England, notice of the marriage must be given to the local superintendent registrar.
- ❑ Choose the hymns, music and readings for the ceremony
- ❑ Choose and order the stationery
- ❑ Book the musicians for the reception
- ❑ Choose a florist and have an initial meeting about the flowers

First Things First
Your Wedding Ceremony
Your Suppliers
Your Reception
Dressed to Thrill
Your Wedding Gifts
Your Honeymoon
One Week and Counting

- ❑ Order the wedding cake
- ❑ Book the wedding transport
- ❑ Arrange dress fittings and shop for bridesmaids' dresses and accessories
- ❑ Chat to your hairdresser about your wedding day hairstyle
- ❑ Begin a beauty regime
- ❑ Book a first night hotel
- ❑ Book your honeymoon
- ❑ Check passports are valid and arrange any inoculations/medication
- ❑ Choose your wedding rings
- ❑ Organise your gift list

Two months before

- ❑ Finalise your order of service and order the printed versions
- ❑ Reconfirm all prior bookings in writing
- ❑ Post invitations with gift list details
- ❑ Buy lingerie and other accessories
- ❑ Check the groom and best man have organised their outfits
- ❑ Choose presents for all your attendants

One month before

- ❑ Book hair and make-up appointments for the morning of the wedding
- ❑ Make sure everyone involved knows what's happening and when
- ❑ Write to banks and other official bodies if you are changing your name
- ❑ Your departure – do you want to make a grand exit?

Two weeks before

- ❑ Try on your full wedding outfit and practise walking in your shoes
- ❑ Confirm guest numbers with your caterer and draw up a seating plan
- ❑ Order currency and travellers' cheques for the honeymoon
- ❑ Enjoy your hen night – and get your groom to hold his stag night

One week before

- ❑ Arrange a rehearsal of the ceremony, if required
- ❑ Confirm all reception arrangements in writing
- ❑ Confirm supplier arrangements (caterer, photographer, video, transport, florist and so on), including timings
- ❑ Make a list of must-take shots for the photographer
- ❑ Make a play list for the DJ, including favourites – and mentioning anything you hate! Also ensure they have the right music for your first dance.
- ❑ Check the groom, best man and your dad are all preparing a speech
- ❑ Think about making a bride's speech

The day before

- ❑ Help to decorate the reception venue, if necessary
- ❑ Arrange for the cake to be delivered to the reception
- ❑ Pack for the honeymoon and have the cases sent to the reception venue
- ❑ Have a manicure and pedicure
- ❑ Relax and have an early night

On the big day

- ❑ Allow plenty of time to get ready
- ❑ Collect/have delivered bouquets and buttonholes
- ❑ Brief the ushers on their role
- ❑ Ensure the best man knows he needs to make sure everyone has transport from the ceremony to the reception

Your notes

Roles and responsibilities

The key questions

Q Who do you want around you? **Weddings are stressful and you'll want to surround yourself with people you can trust to help, particularly if you work full-time. They need to be calm, unflappable and ready to turn their hand to just about anything that comes up.**

Q Who should you choose for bridesmaids? **Not everyone will shine in the spotlight so choose your bridesmaids carefully. Think about their strengths (and weaknesses) and if someone turns you down, don't be offended. It may be that she's too busy to be properly involved or just doesn't fancy taking a leading role.**

Q What about your groom? **Your fiancé should play a key role in his own wedding, supporting you and helping to make major decisions about issues such as the venue, food and the guest list. Just don't expect him to get excited about the colour schemes, favours and the flowers – this is where your girlfriends will be invaluable!**

Q And your mother? **If you have a good relationship with your mum, she's likely to become your most valuable ally, brimming with enthusiasm, advice and great ideas. Just make sure she doesn't take over completely!**

Once you have a good idea of who you would like to play a big part in your wedding, you'll need to have a clear understanding of what they're expected to do so you can brief them properly.

Your chief bridesmaid

Traditionally the bride's sister or her best friend, the chief bridesmaid needs to be someone who is unflappable, organised and there to provide a shoulder to cry on during the ups and downs of planning a wedding.

Her main duties include:

- Supporting the bride at all times, listening to the moans and mopping up any tears.
- Providing a helping hand with whatever jobs need doing.
- Acting as a shopping partner on trips to find the bride's dress and the bridesmaids' outfits.
- Organising a suitably amazing hen night.
- Making sure all the other bridesmaids are dressed properly and know their duties.
- Helping the bride to dress on the big day.
- Following the bride down the aisle and generally making sure she looks gorgeous at all times.
- Standing in the receiving line, if there is one.
- Mingling with guests and making sure everyone is having a good time.
- Helping the bride to change, if she's leaving the reception, and arranging for her dress and any gifts to be taken home.

Your best man

The choice of best man is up to your groom. It's usually his brother or best friend and, if you don't approve of his choice, keep it to yourself! Weddings tend to bring out the best in people and even if you have your doubts, hopefully you'll be pleasantly surprised.

His main duties include:

- Helping the groom and bridal party men to buy or hire their suits.
- Organising a suitably boozy but not too mad stag night.
- Making sure the groom gets to the ceremony in plenty of time (15 minutes before the bride is about right).
- Ensuring any ushers know what they are supposed to do.
- Standing with the groom at the altar as he waits for his bride.
- Keeping the wedding rings safe until they are needed.
- Settling any fees due (for the ceremony, choir and organist, for example) after the ceremony.

- Making sure all the guests have transport from the church to the reception venue.
- Standing in the receiving line, if there is one.
- Mingling with guests and making sure everyone is having a good time.
- Giving a speech after the father of the bride and the groom have finished theirs.
- Arranging for the groom's suit to be returned, if it has been hired.

Your bridesmaids

Bridesmaids can be relatives or friends, old or young. It's entirely up to you and, to a certain extent, the style and formality of the wedding. Usually the bigger and more formal the wedding, the more attendants you'll want.

Think about the mix of personalities – you want everyone to get along – and be clear about what you want them to do. It may be that you only want one flower girl or even no bridesmaids at all. Close friends who could be offended at being excluded can always be given a role, such as doing a reading, so they still feel special.

Their main duties include:

- Offering to help with any pre-wedding tasks that needs doing.
- Helping the chief bridesmaid to organise the hen night.
- Shopping for outfits and accessories (remembering to be flexible and not sulky if the dress isn't their first choice!).
- Helping the bride to organise and dress younger maids on the big day.
- Travelling with the bride's mother and other bridesmaids to the ceremony.
- Walking down the aisle in front of or behind the bride, whichever she prefers. In the US, bridesmaids walk in front, so she's the main event!
- Mingling with the guests and making sure everyone is having a good time.
- Keeping an eye on younger bridesmaids and attendants during the reception and keeping them amused if necessary.

Flower girls and ring bearer

You are guaranteed some great photographs if you involve small children in your wedding. But do remember – little ones, however cute, are unpredictable and won't necessarily follow your carefully made plans.

Flower girls are usually between five and ten years old and walk down the aisle in front of the bride, scattering flower petals from a basket for the bride to walk on. The ring bearer or page boy is usually a small boy aged between four and seven and his role is to walk down the aisle with, or just behind, the flower girls, bearing the wedding rings – perhaps fake rings, just in case! – on an ornate cushion.

Ushers

Usually only part of a church wedding, the ushers are traditionally brothers or close male friends of the bride and groom. If you're having a larger civil wedding, you may well want to enlist the help of some ushers to keep everything moving smoothly. It's their job to ensure that all the guests are seated before the ceremony, the bride's family and friends on the left and the groom's family and friends on the right. They should give each guest an order of service sheet as they arrive and ensure, with the best man, that everyone has transport to the reception once the ceremony is over.

Mother of the bride

Hopefully, your mum will become your best friend as you plan your wedding, providing you with support and wisdom on just about everything from food to flower arrangements. Decide together on what type of role you want your mother to have, which can include any or all of the following:

- Contributing to the wedding budget.
- Helping to source potential suppliers, from the venue to the caterers.
- Compiling the family section of the guest list and helping to cut it back, if necessary.
- Being a shoulder for her daughter to cry on when it all gets too much.

- Shopping for the wedding dress as well as her own outfit.
- Helping to address and post invitations, then tracking the RSVP list.
- Travelling to the ceremony with the bridesmaids.
- Sitting in the pew directly in front of the ceremony. Walking out first after the bride and groom once the ceremony is over.
- Standing in the receiving line, if there is one.
- Sitting at the top table during the meal.
- Dancing with the groom's father and the groom during the evening.
- Making sure all gifts received at the reception are taken home and stored safely.
- Reminding her daughter – at least ten times during the day – how beautiful, wonderful and special she is!

Father of the bride

Traditionally, the bride's dad got to sign cheques, walk his daughter up the aisle and make a speech during the reception, and for many dads this is pretty much all he will want to do – the colour of the trim on the invitations certainly won't be keeping him awake at night! But if he wants to play a bigger part, there's no reason why he shouldn't do many of the same tasks as the bride's mother, including:

- Contributing to the wedding budget.
- Helping to source potential suppliers, from the venue to the caterer.
- Compiling the family section of the guest list and helping to cut it back, if necessary.
- Finding his outfit, including arranging suit hire if necessary.
- Accompanying his daughter to the ceremony, helping to calm her last-minute nerves.
- Walking his daughter down the aisle and giving her away.

- Sitting in the pew directly in front of the ceremony. Walking out first after the bride and groom once the ceremony is over.
- Standing in the receiving line, if there is one.
- Sitting at the top table during the meal.
- Giving a simple speech, thanking everyone for coming, proposing a toast and then introducing the groom to give his speech.
- Dancing with the groom's mother and the bride during the evening.
- Staying until the end of the evening, ensuring everything is paid for and, if clearing up is part of the deal, that this has been done.

Mother and father of the groom

As wedding finances change, things are changing here. Traditionally, the groom's parents don't play a big part in their son's wedding but these days, with them perhaps contributing an equal share of the wedding budget, there's no reason why they shouldn't be just as involved as the bride's parents (see the lists of duties for the mother and father of the bride above). Obviously, the groom's father won't walk the bride up the aisle and is unlikely to give a speech unless you want him to. Chat their role through at the outset and agree between you where you would like them to be involved.

Other leading roles

You may find you have special people among your family and friends who you want to single out in some particular way. One way to involve valued friends who aren't suited to a leading role is to ask them to give a reading. Short poems and meaningful readings are an important party of any ceremony, whether civil or religious, and can make all the difference to the mood of the day. Anyone chosen to give a reading needs to be a confident speaker with a loud, clear voice and will need to practise beforehand.

You could also ask a musically talented friend to play or sing during the ceremony and this always adds a lovely personal touch to the day. Again, just make sure he or she is up to it. Performing in your living room is one thing; singing in front of a church full of people is quite another!

First Things First
Your Wedding Ceremony
Your Suppliers
Your Reception
Dressed to Thrill
Your Wedding Gifts
Your Honeymoon
One Week and Counting

Your attendants' details

Write down contact details for the bridesmaids and other attendants so you always know where to find them.

Chief bridesmaid

Name

Home | Work

Mobile | E-mail

Best man

Name

Home | Work

Mobile | E-mail

Bridesmaid

Name

Home | Work

Mobile | E-mail

Bridesmaid

Name

Home | Work

Mobile | E-mail

Bridesmaid

Name

Home | Work

Mobile | E-mail

Usher

Name

Home | Work

Mobile | E-mail

Usher

Name

Home | Work

Mobile | E-mail

Usher

Name

Home | Work

Mobile | E-mail

Flower girl

Name

Home number | Parents' e-mail

Ring bearer/page boy

Name

Home number | Parents' e-mail

Ceremony reader

Name

Home | Work

Mobile | E-mail

Soloist

Name

Home | Work

Mobile | E-mail

Your guest list

The key questions

Q Who should be invited? **Accept early on that you won't be able to invite everyone you would like to your wedding. The venue may not be big enough and you probably can't afford it. If numbers need limiting, look at not inviting workmates' partners and maybe having a child-free reception.**

Q How big is your budget? **The reception takes the biggest slice of the wedding budget and you need to think of each guest as having a price tag on their head. You don't want to appear mean, but you have to ask yourselves just how important it is to have each person on the list with you on your special day.**

Q What is the mood of the wedding? **Do you want big and formal or small and intimate? The style of your wedding dictates how many people you'll want to attend. If you like the idea of a lot of guests but have a limited budget, think about having a cocktail and canapés reception rather than an expensive sit-down meal.**

Unless you have an unlimited budget, deciding on the guest list is going to be an exercise in tact and diplomacy. So how do you decide who gets an invitation? Traditionally the guest list is split 50/50 between the bride and her family and the groom and his family. But it's often not as straightforward as that and you'll need to take other factors into consideration.

The size of the venue

The number of guests you can invite will be determined by the size of your venue. An average-sized banqueting suite or hotel ballroom can accommodate 100–150 seated for dinner. Most marquees can seat around 100 guests. If you want anything bigger, your choice of venue will be limited to very large – and often very expensive – hotels.

How big is your family?

If you or your groom has a large family and you want to invite them all, three-quarters of your guest list could be filled even before you start thinking about workmates and other friends. Your parents will want to invite family and if they are paying the majority of the wedding bill, you'll have to listen to their wishes. If this sounds familiar, then you'll have to think about compromising somewhere along the line.

What's your budget?

At the planning stage, you have to be realistic about how much you can afford. It's no good thinking you can invite everyone if you don't have a big budget. Think of each guest as a sum of money: the more guests you invite, the more you have to pay – it's that simple – so think carefully about your numbers. You could leave out the partners of work colleagues or have an adults-only wedding, asking friends and relatives to leave their children at home. You could also cut costs by thinking about having a pay bar once the formal part of the reception is over.

You should expect approximately 10–15 per cent of your invited guests to decline, for one reason or another, so you can either have a B-list of invitees ready or accept that you can save some cash on the numbers and spend it somewhere else.

Small can be beautiful

Being the focus of attention at a huge wedding sends shivers down the spine of many couples, so a small celebration with close friends and family with a blow-out lunch will be much more appealing than a major event. It's your day and people will understand if you tell them that is really what you want. You can always have a party to celebrate your first month of married life without the fuss and formality.

First Things First
Your Wedding Ceremony
Your Suppliers
Your Reception
Dressed to Thrill
Your Wedding Gifts
Your Honeymoon
One Week and Counting

WEDDING WORKSHEET

The guest list

This is your essential guest list manager of who will be coming to your wedding.

Guests	Invited	RSVP	Dietaryrequirements
Name			
Name			
Children			
Name			
Name			
Children			
Name			
Name			
Children			
Name			
Name			
Children			
Name			
Name			
Children			
Name			
Name			
Children			
Name			
Name			
Children			

Guests	Invited	RSVP	Dietaryrequirements
Name			
Name			
Children			
Name			
Name			
Children			
Name			
Name			
Children			
Name			
Name			
Children			
Name			
Name			
Children			
Name			
Name			
Children			
Name			
Name			
Children			
Name			
Name			
Children			

Guests	Invited	RSVP	Dietaryrequirements
Name			
Name			
Children			
Name			
Name			
Children			
Name			
Name			
Children			
Name			
Name			
Children			
Name			
Name			
Children			
Name			
Name			
Children			
Name			
Name			
Children			
Name			
Name			
Children			

Guests	Invited	RSVP	Dietaryrequirements
Name			
Name			
Children			
Name			
Name			
Children			
Name			
Name			
Children			
Name			
Name			
Children			
Name			
Name			
Children			
Name			
Name			
Children			
Name			
Name			
Children			
Name			
Name			
Children			

Guests	Invited	RSVP	Dietaryrequirements
Name			
Name			
Children			
Name			
Name			
Children			
Name			
Name			
Children			
Name			
Name			
Children			
Name			
Name			
Children			
Name			
Name			
Children			
Name			
Name			
Children			
Name			
Name			
Children			

Summary notes to date

You may not have finalised your decisions on everything, but it should help to have all your thoughts on one page.

Proposed date

Timings

Estimated budget

Estimated number of guests

Favourite venue(s)

Style of reception (sit-down, buffet or canapés)

Your notes

Chapter 2

Your Wedding Ceremony

The setting, the words, the readings and the music – the essential elements that must come together for that all-important moment when you say 'I do' and become husband and wife

The key questions

Q Do you want a religious wedding? If you and your family are regular churchgoers and neither of you has been married before, the obvious choice is to marry in your local place of worship. If either of you is divorced, having a religious ceremony is much more difficult and you'll need to seek advice. The same applies if you are contemplating a mixed faith wedding; it is possible but you need to know the facts before you start planning anything.

Q Is a civil wedding right for you? Civil weddings are currently the popular choice for marriage in the UK. The informality is what appeals to most couples and, with the advent of being able to marry in a licensed building, having the ceremony and reception in one place makes the day simpler to co-ordinate – and there's a lot to be said for that!

Q How much can you personalise the ceremony? If you are having a religious ceremony, you are pretty much bound by the traditional order of service, though you can add your own choice of readings and music to make your day more personal to the two of you. The civil ceremony allows much more flexibility and, providing you consult the registrar, you can even write some of your own vows.

If you are getting married in England, Wales or Northern Ireland, you have two choices: a religious ceremony in a church, synagogue or chapel; or a civil wedding in a licensed building or register office. Weddings in Scotland are governed by a different set of laws, but we'll cover that later.

Over half of all weddings in the UK are currently non-religious but it's totally up to you and your fiancé and whether you have any religious convictions. Sit down with him and decide which type of ceremony is right for you. If you have any doubts, make appointments with the local registrar and your local minister and chat through the options.

The legalities

To be legally married in the UK you need to comply with the following:

- You and your fiancé must be at least 16 years old (in England, Wales and Northern Ireland, if either of you is under 18, one parent or guardian must give consent).
- You must not be closely related.
- In England, Wales and Northern Ireland the marriage must take place in premises where the ceremony can be legally solemnised (register office, premises licensed for marriage, or a parish church or other place of worship registered for marriage). In Scotland you can marry anywhere providing there is a minister and witnesses present.
- The ceremony must take place in the presence of a registrar or another authorised person such as a priest or rabbi.
- In England, Wales and Northern Ireland, the ceremony must take place between 8am and 6pm. In Scotland there are no time restrictions.
- Two witnesses must be present.
- You must both be free and eligible to marry.

In England, Wales and Northern Ireland you can't get married outdoors, for example on the beach or in a garden where no specific address for the ceremony can be given. In Scotland you can get married wherever you like and have either a religious or civil ceremony in the place of your choosing, including outside, as long as you have the officiant and two witnesses.

Religious ceremonies

The key questions

Q Is a religious ceremony what you want? **There was a time when a religious marriage ceremony was the automatic choice for just about every couple, but not any more. Think hard about whether the commitments involved in a religious ceremony are meaningful to you, or would you be doing it just for your parents? If you do have doubts, talk them through with your family, explaining that you feel that the marriage ceremony must reflect your own beliefs, whatever they may be. Get advice from your vicar or priest, who may be able to make things clearer.**

The ceremony – useful contacts list

Baptists Union	01235 517700	
British Humanist Association	020 7079 3580	www.humanism.org.uk
Church of England	020 7898 1000	www.cofe.anglican.org
Church of Scotland	01312 255722	
General Register Office (GRO) for England and Wales	01514 714200	www.ons.gov.uk
GRO for Guernsey	01481 725277	
GRO for Jersey	01534 502335	
GRO for Northern Ireland	02890 252000	
GRO for Scotland	01313 144447	
Greek Archdiocese	020 7723 4787	www.nosts.com/church
Jewish Marriage Council	020 8203 6311	
Methodist Church	020 7222 8010	
United Reform Church	020 7916 2020	

Q How do you find out what is involved? **It's important that you find out as much as possible about every type of marriage ceremony so make an appointment to see your minister or rabbi. They will be happy to answer all your questions about what is actually involved.**

Q Can you make the ceremony more personal? **The traditional religious marriage ceremony has remained largely unchanged for many years and you won't be allowed a lot of freedom to alter the majority of the order of service. Where you can add some personal touches is through musical choices and with the addition of readings that you feel say something about you both. Do your research and then ask your minister for advice, because ultimately it's up to him or her what you can and cannot include.**

A Church of England ceremony

To get married in your local church, one of you needs to live in the parish and be on the electoral roll. You don't have to attend church regularly, although some ministers may insist on it so do check first.

Part of the legal requirement is that the minister reads out the banns – the public announcement of your intention to marry – in the church on three consecutive Sundays, following which the marriage must take place within three months. You usually both attend church on at least one of these occasions to hear your banns being read. If one of you lives in a different parish, you need to arrange for the banns to read there too, though it doesn't have to be on the same Sundays.

If you don't live in the parish of the church you want to marry in and you are not on the electoral register, you'll need to apply for a special licence from the Archbishop of Canterbury showing a long-standing connection with the preferred church. Just being close to your reception venue is not a good enough reason!

If either of you is divorced and your former partner is still alive you'll find it difficult to have a full marriage service in a Church of England church. Some ministers may make an exception, but it will always be decided on the basis of the individual circumstances. An alternative is to have a register office ceremony first followed by a church blessing.

At the time of going to press, the costs for a Church of England wedding are £18 for the publication of the banns and a further £12 for a certificate of banns. The marriage service costs £218 and the marriage certificate is £7.

If you want bell ringers, charges vary but you can expect to pay about £100 for this service. A choir costs anything from £50 to £150 and a soloist about the same again. There may also be a small location hire fee, a charge for an organist and in winter a small charge for additional heating.

A Roman Catholic ceremony

Roman Catholic wedding requirements are much the same as those for a Church of England wedding. You should organise a meeting with your priest as early as possible after your engagement, and take your baptism and confirmation certificates with you. Most priests are empowered to act as registrars so the civil aspect of the wedding is covered at the same time.

If both of you are Roman Catholic, the ceremony is usually part of a Nuptial Mass where you both receive communion, though you can choose to be married without a full Mass. If one of you is not Catholic, you'll need a dispensation from the priest for a 'mixed marriage'; in this case, you won't include a Mass in the ceremony.

The Roman Catholic Church does not allow the remarriage of divorcees. Exceptions are occasionally made if your first marriage wasn't recognised by the Church, but you should consult your priest for advice.

Other religions

For all religious weddings other than Church of England or Roman Catholic, the legal requirements are the same as for civil ceremonies and you need to apply to the religious authority at your place of worship as well as the local superintendent registrar. To find out more and for information on inter-faith marriages, see the Useful Contacts box on page 49 for who can help you.

The Christian wedding ceremony

A traditional Christian marriage ceremony has followed much the same basic format for many years, but you can make it unique to you with your choice of readings, favourite hymns and music. Talk to the minister about your options as they will prove a mine of information, and you do need them to agree to what you would like to include. If you feel uncomfortable with a particular phrase in the service, ask about the possibility of making a change. Most modern brides prefer to say 'love, honour and cherish' rather than 'obey'. And most couples now both promise to bestow all their worldly goods; it used to be only the groom who offered this!

You usually give your guests an order of service sheet as they arrive at the ceremony so they can follow proceedings and it's a good idea to include the words of hymns – you can't be sure everyone will know them and it sounds so much better if everyone sings along. Your minister will be able to tell you if you need copyright clearance to print the words of any hymns on your order of service. A small fee is payable to the copyright holder for the use of any words for the 70 years following the death of the writer, but this doesn't apply if you just want to sing the hymns or use a hymn book.

For a religious ceremony, an organist usually supplies the music, or perhaps a choir or even a string quartet. If you want something more modern to accompany you down the aisle, most churches have the facility for playing a CD but, again, do check first that your musical choices are acceptable to your minister. Remember, you are in a place of worship.

Religious order of service

This is the traditional order of service to complete as you plan your ideal ceremony.

Entrance of the bride

Musical accompaniment

Introduction by the minister

Hymn 1

The marriage ceremony

Prayers

Reading 1

Reader

Hymn 2

Reading 2

Reader

Optional musical performance

Chosen music

Performers

Conclusion of the marriage ceremony

Signing of the register

Musical accompaniment

Recessional (exit of the bride and groom)

Musical accompaniment

Your Wedding Ceremony
Your Suppliers
Your Reception
Dressed to Thrill
Your Wedding Gifts
Your Honeymoon
One Week and Counting

Civil ceremonies

The key questions

Q Why would you have a civil ceremony? **This type of wedding now accounts for over half of all weddings in the UK and it's a growing trend. Couples choose a civil marriage ceremony for many reasons but largely because of lack of religious conviction, because their relationship involves mixed faiths or because one or other partner has divorced. A civil ceremony is quick and simple and in the case of a register office ceremony can be over in about 10 minutes, which also appeals to couples who want the minimum of fuss.**

Q What are the options? **You have two main options for a civil ceremony, either holding it in your local register office or in a building that is licensed for marriage. In either case you'll be married by the local registrar and the ceremony will have no religious connotations.**

Q Where can you find out more? **A civil ceremony is arranged through the register office in your local district and the contact details can be found through your council offices. Many districts have very helpful websites that will answer most of your questions but, if you want to know more, make an appointment with the registrar, who will be happy to help with your queries.**

Civil ceremonies

If you don't want to have a religious ceremony or can't because of divorce or mixed faith, then the alternative is a civil wedding. You can choose from either a register office ceremony or a ceremony performed in a building that holds a marriage licence. In either case, the process for arranging everything is the same.

Firstly, you need to contact the superintendent registrar for your district, which you must have lived in for a minimum of seven days. Even if both of you live in the same district, each of you needs your own superintendent registrar's certificate so both bride and groom must apply in person to the local office. You then wait 15 days for the certificate to be issued and this is valid for 12 months.

Use this first appointment to check that your preferred date is free and that a registrar is free to attend your venue if you want to have a wedding in a licensed building. This is very important and you should never book your venue until you know that the registrar is able to marry you on a particular date. If you are marrying out of your local district, you'll need to speak to the superintendent registrar for the area where you want to get married about booking a ceremony.

If you haven't yet decided on a venue for your wedding, you can ask the registrar for a list of local licensed premises. If you want a complete list of over 3,000 countrywide premises licensed for marriage visit www.gro.gov.uk/gro/content/marriages, which will let you obtain a printout of the full list for a small fee.

It currently costs £30 per person to give notice of your marriage. Fees for a register office wedding range from about £40 on weekdays to about £250 at weekends. Civil ceremonies at a licensed venue are more expensive and cost up to £400 at weekends, though prices vary considerably around the country. You also have to pay £7 for the marriage certificate at either type of ceremony.

Personalising your civil wedding ceremony

You have more scope to personalise proceedings for a civil, rather than a religious, ceremony – you can even write many of your own vows, if you would like to. Just remember, a civil wedding is still a legal undertaking and anything you want to include should reflect the solemnity of the occasion. Keep anything too personal or slightly jokey vows for a private moment between the two of you.

Legally, a civil wedding cannot have vows, songs, poems or readings that have any religious references – and this can even mean words like 'angel' in some cases – so it's very important that you check everything you want to include with your registrar before the wedding. You generally won't be able to bring in anything that extends the ceremony beyond a total of about 20 minutes, sometimes even shorter if you are having a register office ceremony.

The informal nature of the civil ceremony is what attracts many couples but you should think about adding a few readings or poems, otherwise the whole thing could be over so quickly that your guests will hardly have taken their seats before you have said your vows and you are man and wife.

If you are marrying in a licensed premises, the order of service can follow pretty much the same format as for a religious ceremony; it's just the words that are different and, of course, there are no hymns or prayers. A register office ceremony is usually much simpler but most locations will have a CD player to play your favourite music as you enter and leave.

Writing your own vows

If you want to make your civil wedding ceremony truly personal, you can have a go at writing your own vows. To get you started, think about what marriage means to you and what it will bring to your life – things such as love, respect, friendship, loyalty and trust – but don't make it too cute or too personal. You'll probably be limited to about three minutes of speaking time and will have to run everything past the registrar before you commit to anything.

Once the wording has been agreed, make sure you practise a few times before the wedding so you are familiar with the words and can look at one another rather than at a piece of paper as you exchange your vows.

How to personalise your ceremony

The registrar introduces the bride and groom to their guests and welcomes them to the happy occasion. The bride begins by offering a vow to her groom, for example:

> *We are here today to make a lasting commitment to one another. I want the world to know that you bring joy to my life. I affirm the special bond between us and promise from this day forward to be your confidante, your best friend and to share all your hopes and dreams.*
>
> *In recognition of this, I .... take you .... to be my husband. With this vow I promise to be a loyal and trustworthy wife and to love you whatever the circumstances.*

The groom says similar words about his commitment to his bride. The reading of an appropriate text or poem can be inserted at this point. The ceremony then follows the traditional route of wedding vows, the exchange of rings and the pronouncement (when you become man and wife).

Adding that special personal touch

- Walk up the aisle with both sets of parents.
- Include the names of deceased relatives or friends somewhere in the ceremony.
- Face the congregation/guests to say your vows, with the officiant having his or her back to the audience.
- Give all your guests a candle to hold as you say your vows (if the venue will allow it).
- If it's a small wedding, get everyone to gather around you as you say your vows.
- For complete freedom, think about a humanist ceremony. For details contact The British Humanist Association, see page 49.

Civil ceremony order of service

This is the traditional order of service to complete as you plan your ideal ceremony.

Entrance of the bride

Musical accompaniment

Introduction by the officiant

Reading 1

Reader

The marriage ceremony

Reading 2

Reader

Optional musical performance

Chosen music

Performers

Conclusion of the marriage ceremony

Signing of the register

Musical accompaniment

Recessional (exit of the bride and groom)

Musical accompaniment

Music and readings

The key questions

Q Where can you find inspiration for your ceremony? If you are having a religious ceremony, the best person to ask for general advice is your minister or rabbi, who'll have lots of suggestions for hymns and reading options.

For a civil ceremony, where you have more choices, you can use websites (www.youandyourwedding.co.uk has a good vows and readings section) and check out your local library, where you'll find a host of books devoted to quotations and readings for weddings. The local music shop will also stock CDs of wedding music if you need to hear some of the more popular choices for both types of ceremony.

Q Can anything be chosen? You'll need to check all choices of readings and music with either the minister (if you are having a religious ceremony) or the registrar (if yours is a civil ceremony). A civil ceremony does allow more freedom but your choices still have to reflect the solemnity of the occasion. And remember that anything used in a civil ceremony must not have any religious connotations.

Q Who gives the readings? Readings are an important part of any style of marriage ceremony. You need to choose the person giving a reading carefully and, while it's considered an honour to be asked, public speaking isn't for everyone. The speaker must have a confident voice and be able to speak clearly and slowly. Make sure whoever is chosen practises their words beforehand; this will help their confidence and ensure they look up, at least occasionally, and address their audience.

Traditional music for a religious ceremony

Arrival of the guests:

Jesu, Joy of Man's Desiring – *Bach*
Water Music – *Handel*
Pastoral Symphony, Messiah – *Handel*
Canon in D – *Pachelbel*

Entrance of the bride:

Trumpet Voluntary – *Clarke*
The Arrival of the Queen of Sheba – *Handel*
Trumpet Tune in D – *Purcell*
Grand March from Aïda – *Verdi*
Spring/The Four Seasons – *Vivaldi*
Bridal Chorus from Lohengrin
(Here Comes the Bride) – *Wagner*

Signing of the register:

Cantique de Jean Racine – *Fauré*
Laudate Dominum – *Mozart*
The Lord Bless You and Keep You – *Rutter*
Ave Maria – *Schubert*
Spring/The Four Seasons – *Vivaldi*

Recessional:

Hallelujah Chorus – *Handel*
Wedding March from A Midsummer Night's Dream – *Mendelssohn*
Radetsky March – *Strauss*
The Grand March from Aïda – *Verdi*
The Ride of the Valkyries – *Wagner*
Toccata from Symphony No 5 – *Widor*

Traditional hymns for a religious ceremony

Lead Us, Heavenly Father, Lead Us

Lead us, Heavenly Father, lead us,
O'er the world's tempestuous sea.
Guard us, guide us, keep us, feed us,
For we have no help but thee.
Yet possessing every blessing
If our God the Father be.

Love Divine, All Loves Excelling

Love divine, all loves excelling.
Joy to heaven, to earth come down.
Fix in us thy humble dwelling,
All thy faithful mercies crown.

Jesus, Thou art all compassion,
Pure unbounded love Thou art.
Visit us with Thy salvation,
Enter every trembling heart.

At The Name of Jesus

At the name of Jesus
Every knee shall bow,
Every tongue confess Him,
King of Glory now.

All People That On Earth Do Dwell

All people that on earth do dwell,
Sing to the Lord with cheerful voice.
Serve Him with joy, His praises tell.
Come now before Him and rejoice.

Immortal, Invisible

Immortal, invisible, God only wise.
In light inaccessible, hid from our eyes.
Most blessed, most glorious
The ancient of days,
Almighty, victorious,
Thy great name we praise.

Praise My Soul, The King of Heaven

Praise my soul, the King of Heaven,
To His feet thy tribute bring;
Ransomed, healed, restored, forgiven,
Who like me His praise would sing?
Praise Him, praise Him, praise Him, praise Him,
Praise the everlasting King.

The Lord's My Shepherd (Psalm 23)

The Lord's my shepherd; I'll not want.
He maketh me down to lie
In pastures green; He leadeth me
The quiet waters by.

Dear Lord and Father of Mankind

Dear Lord and Father of mankind,
Forgive our foolish ways.
Re-clothe us in our rightful mind,
In purer lives Thy service find,
In deeper reverence praise,
In deeper reverence praise.

Traditional religious readings

Appropriate Bible readings

On husbands and wives

- Proverbs 17; 20:25–29; 31:10–13
- Ephesians 5:28–33
- Ruth 1:16
- Genesis 2:18–24
- Song of Solomon 4:1–3; 5:10–14; 7

On marriage

- Hebrews 13:4
- Ecclesiastes 4:9–12
- Matthew 19:4–6
- Mark 10:6–9
- John 2:1–11

On home and family

- Matthew 7:21,24–27
- Ephesians 3:14–19
- Proverbs 24:3–6

On praise and joy

- Psalms 23; 33; 34; 63; 90; 100; 103; 139; 145; 150
- Isaiah 61:10–11
- Jeremiah 33:10–11
- John 15:9–17

On love

- John 15:9–17
- I Corinthians 13:1–13
- Ephesians 4:1–4; 5:1–2
- Matthew 22: 35–40
- Romans 12:1–2; 9–18
- Proverbs 3:3–6
- I Peter 3:7

Other readings for a religious ceremony

From Hamlet (Shakespeare)

Doubt thou the stars are fire;
Doubt that the sun doth move;
Doubt truth be a liar;
But never doubt I love.

Sonnet 116 (Shakespeare)

Let me not to the marriage of true minds
Admit impediments. Love is not love
Which alters when it alteration finds,
Or bends with the remover to remove:
Oh no! It is an ever-fixed mark.
That looks on tempests and is never shaken;
It is the star to every wandering bark,
Whose worth's unknown, although his height be taken.
Love's not Time's fool, though rosy lips and cheeks
Within his bending sickle's compass come:
Love alters not with his brief hours and weeks,
But bears it out even to the edge of doom.
If this be error and upon me proved,
I never writ, nor no man ever loved.

Irish Blessing

May the road rise to meet you.
May the wind be always on your back.
May the sun shine warm upon your face,
The rains fall soft upon your fields.
And until we meet again,
May God hold you in the palm of His hand.

May God be with you and bless you.
May you see your children's children.
May you be poor in misfortune,
Rich in blessings.
May you know nothing but happiness
From this day forward.

May the road rise to meet you.
May the wind be always on your back.
May the warm rays of sun fall upon your home.
And may the hand of a friend always be near.

May green be the grass you walk on.
May blue be the skies above you.
May pure be the joys that surround you.
May true be the hearts that love you.

The Prophet (Kahlil Gibran)

Love has no other desire but to fulfil itself.
But if you love and must needs have desires, let these be your desires;
To melt and be like a running brook that sings its melody to the night;
To know the pain of too much tenderness;
To be wounded by your own understanding of love
And to bleed willingly and joyfully.
To wake at dawn with a winged heart and give thanks for another day of loving;
To rest at the noon hour and meditate love's ecstasy;
To return home at eventide with gratitude
And then to sleep with a prayer for the beloved in your heart and a song of praise on your lips.

How Do I Love Thee? (Elizabeth Barrett Browning)

How do I love thee? Let me count the ways.
I love thee to the depth and breadth and height
My soul can reach, when feeling out of sight
For the ends of being an Ideal Grace.
I love thee to the level of every day's
Most quiet need, by sun and candlelight.
I love thee freely, as men strive for Right;
I love thee purely, as they turn from Praise.
I love thee with the passion put to use
In my old griefs, and with my childhood's faith.
I love thee with a love I seemed to lose
With my lost saints, I love thee with the breath,
Smiles, tears, of all my life! And if God choose,
I shall but love thee better after death.

Classical music for a civil ceremony

Arrival of the guests:	Water Music – *Handel* Canon in D – *Pachelbel*
Entrance of the bride:	Prince of Denmark's March – *Clarke* Trumpet Tune in D – *Purcell* Bridal Chorus from Lohengrin (Here Comes the Bride) – *Wagner*
Signing of the register:	Air on a G String – *Bach* Chanson de Matin – *Elgar* Movements/Divertimenti – *Mozart*
Recessional:	Wedding March from A Midsummer Night's Dream – *Mendelssohn* Spring/The Four Seasons – *Vivaldi*

Contemporary music for a civil ceremony

Always and Forever	*Heatwave*
Can't Help Falling in Love	*Elvis Presley*
Circle of Life	*Elton John*
Endless Love	*Diana Ross*
Gravity of Love	*Enigma*
Have I Told You Lately	*Van Morrison*
It Had to be You	*Harry Connick Jr*
Just the Way You Are	*Richard Clayderman*
Love and Marriage	*Frank Sinatra*
Lovely Day	*Bill Withers*
Loving You	*Kenny G*
Only You	*The Platters*
Somewhere Only We Know	*Keane*
Take My Breath Away	*Berlin*
Unchained Melody	*The Righteous Brothers*
Unforgettable	*Nat King Cole*
We've Only Just Begun	*The Carpenters*
When a Man Loves a Woman	*Percy Sledge*
You to Me Are Everything	*The Real Thing*
You're Beautiful	*James Blunt*

Musical inspiration from the movies

Beauty and the Beast	*Beauty and The Beast*
Everything I Do	*Bryan Adams, Robin Hood*
Happy Days	*Happy Days*
Hopelessly Devoted to You	*Grease*
Love Is All Around	*Four Weddings and a Funeral*
Love Story	*Love Story*
My Heart Will Go On	*Titanic*
So This is Love	*Cinderella*
A Whole New World	*Aladdin*

Readings and poems for a civil ceremony

To My Bride (Steven Reiser)

To my bride, I give you my heart
Sharing love each day, from the very start.
To my bride, I give you my kiss
Filling each day with joy and bliss.
To my bride I give you my mind
Learning each day to be more kind.
To my bride I give you my soul
Growing together to be more whole.
To my bride I give you my life
Rejoicing each day that you are my wife.

Our Great Adventure (Pamela Dugdale)

We are today still dizzy with the astonishment of love.
We are surrounded by affection – by smiles and kindliness,
By flowers and music and gifts and celebration.
Yet they enclose a silence
Where we are close with one another.
My eyes see only you.
I hear nothing but the words
We speak to one another.
This is the day we start our life together.
This is our new beginning.

I Ching

When two people are at one
in their inmost hearts,
they shatter even the strength of iron or bronze.
And when two people understand each other
in their inmost hearts,

their words are sweet and strong,
like the fragrance of orchids.

Eskimo Love Song (Author unknown)
You are my husband/wife.
My feet shall run because of you.
My feet dance because of you.
My heart shall beat because of you.
My eyes see because of you.
My mind thinks because of you.
And I shall love, because of you.

Cherokee Prayer (Traditional)
We honour Mother Earth
And ask for our marriage to be abundant and grow stronger through the seasons.
We honour Fire
And ask that our union be warm and glowing with love in our hearts.
We honour Wind
And ask that we sail through life safe and calm in our father's arms.
We honour Water
To clean and soothe our relationship that it may never thirst for love.

Married Love (Kuan Tao-Sheng)
You and I
Have so much love
That it burns like a fire
In which we bake a lump of clay
Moulded into a figure of you
And a figure of me.
Then we take both of them
And break them into pieces
And mix the pieces with water

And mould again a figure of you
And a figure of me.
I am in your clay;
You are in my clay.
In life we share a single quilt;
In death we will share one coffin.

On Your Wedding Day (Anon)
Today is a day you'll always remember,
The greatest in anyone's life.
You'll start off the day just two people in love
And end it as husband and wife.

It's a brand new beginning, the start of a journey
With moments to cherish and treasure,
And although there'll be times when you both disagree
These will surely be outweighed by pleasure.

You'll have heard many words of advice in the past
When the secrets of marriage were spoken,
But you know that the answers lie hidden inside
Where the bond of true love lies unbroken.

So live happy forever as lovers and friends.
It's the dawn of a new life for you.
As you stand there together with love in your eyes
From the moment you whisper 'I do'.

And with luck all your hopes and your dreams can be real.
May success find its way to your hearts.
Tomorrow can bring you the greatest of joys
But today is the day it all starts.

Getting married abroad

The key questions

Q Is a wedding abroad right for you? **Getting married outside the UK is becoming more and more popular and appeals to couples who have been married before or who simply want something informal in an often amazing location. A wedding abroad is usually a cost-effective way of marrying but you'll have to accept that a lot of family and friends won't be able to join because of financial or time constraints (which may, or may not be a good thing!).**

Q Who does all the planning and paperwork? **The weddings abroad market is growing and most of the major tour operators have a specialist department to arrange everything for you. If you want to get married in Europe there is also a host of wedding planners specialising in countries such as Italy who have excellent local contacts with venues and suppliers. The actual paperwork for most countries is straightforward and no more complicated than a marriage in the UK, although it's always a good idea to get expert advice.**

Q Will it be absolutely legal? **Providing the ceremony is legal in the country in which it's being performed and all the necessary paperwork has been completed, you'll be legally married under UK law. You don't have to register your marriage on your return home but do make sure you keep a copy of your marriage certificate safe for future reference.**

Tying the knot abroad is now a popular choice, especially if you fancy something different, or for second weddings, mixed faith couples, and older couples who don't want the fuss of a traditional big day. Some of the favourite locations are Australia, The Caribbean, Cyprus, Greece, Italy, Malta, Mauritius, Sri Lanka, Thailand and the USA.

Most major tour operators have a weddings department with specialists who can give you expert advice and make all the arrangements. The paperwork involved will vary slightly depending on the country you choose, so although it's fairly straightforward, it's a good idea to consult a professional to ensure you have everything covered. You can arrange a civil or religious ceremony in most destinations, and this will be valid in the UK as long as it's legally recognised in the country in which it takes place. If you have any queries, check with your local register office or contact the tourist board of the country you intend to visit.

Since the recent relaxation in European marriage law, and with increasingly affordable flights, Europe has become one of the favourite locations for a wedding abroad. It is possible to have a weekend wedding accompanied by a large group of guests for much the same budget as for a UK wedding – with sunshine virtually guaranteed!

If you decide you'd like a wedding abroad, you need to do your research first. Most of the major resorts offer a wedding package, often combined with a honeymoon, so find out exactly what's included in the price and what will cost extra. The basic package usually includes all paperwork, the ceremony, a bouquet, a buttonhole for the groom, sparkling wine for a toast, a wedding cake and a photographer.

Most resorts offer a civil ceremony at the hotel but can arrange a religious ceremony or a blessing in a local church if you prefer. Many have an on-site wedding co-ordinator to help ensure that it all goes smoothly once you arrive.

The wedding abroad

It helps to make checklist of things you'll need to think about if you plan a wedding abroad.

Tour operator

Contact name

Telephone

E-mail

Legalities

Passports

Birth certificates

Divorce papers (if applicable)

Hotel details

Contact name

Telephone

E-mail

Website

Wedding package details

Ceremony location

Ceremony decoration	Bride's bouquet
Wedding cake	Champagne for toast
Photographer	Wedding dinner

Other

Estimated budget

Hotel	£
Flights	£
Wedding package	£
Extras	£

The ceremony details

Whatever the location, note down everything you want for the most memorable ceremony.

Name of the location

Location address

Location fees

Name of the celebrant

Contact details

Fees

Choir or musicians

Contact details

Fees

Organist

Contact details

Fee

Music for the guests' arrival

Music for the bride's entrance

Hymn 1

Hymn 2

Hymn 3

Reading 1

Contact details

Chosen reading

Reading 2

Contact details

Chosen reading

Musical performance

Performers

Contact details

Fee

Chosen music for signing the register

Chosen music for the recessional

Your notes

Invitation
Invitation
Invitation

Your Suppliers

You want to organise your wedding with the minimum of stress so it is essential to surround yourself with a team of experts who will hold your hand every step of the way. But who can you trust with these important roles?

The key questions

Q Whose help do you need? Suppliers are anyone you pay to be involved in your wedding – the venue, caterers, florist, stationery company, photographer and so on. They are experienced professionals whose job it is to take your ideas and turn them into reality, hopefully on time and on budget with minimum stress to you!

Q How do you find them? Recommendation is always a great way to find a trustworthy company. Ask anyone who has recently had or been to a wedding about what impressed them most. Also look for suppliers at local wedding fairs and in the back section of wedding magazines. When you have a shortlist, take up references from recent brides to find out what they liked – and what they didn't. Quiz potential venues about who they have worked with in the past. Look at the countrywide supplier directory at www.youandyourwedding.co.uk.

Q How do you get value for money? You probably won't be used to dealing with a project as big or as expensive as a wedding, which is why it's important you trust the people you use. Give suppliers as much information as possible so they can really understand your vision. Pay attention to all their suggestions and get everything discussed confirmed in writing with dates, timings, prices and specifics such as the type of flowers and menu. Speak up when something isn't as you would like.

Q How can you make best use of the budget? **There are lots of companies looking to take your money so make sure you shop around for the best deals on offer. Be clear from the outset what you have to spend and don't be bullied into spending more money unless it seems absolutely necessary.**

Save yourself a lot of time and energy by telephone screening potential suppliers. Arm yourself with a checklist of questions and have a good look at their websites to see room details, lists of services, sample prices and recent examples of their work. See Your Wedding Address Book, pages 214-220.

The overall look and feel of a company website is a great first impression of that supplier's image. Does it look contemporary or traditional (or downright old fashioned)? Once you like what you've seen and heard, and presuming they are free around your proposed dates, then you can make an appointment to take the next step.

Check the details

If your day is going to go perfectly, there's no room for error and the right paperwork goes a long way towards ensuring the professionals you've chosen come through on the day. Every couple needs to be clear about what they want and to confirm everything in writing. Read everything carefully and don't sign until you are completely satisfied it's a reflection of everything you've discussed at your initial meetings. Be sure all the basic details are included such as names, addresses, dates, specific rooms, services to be provided, timings, costs (including VAT) and agreed extras. Make sure you keep a copy of all receipts and correspondence as proof of any payments made for deposits.

As a final reminder, do take out some form of wedding

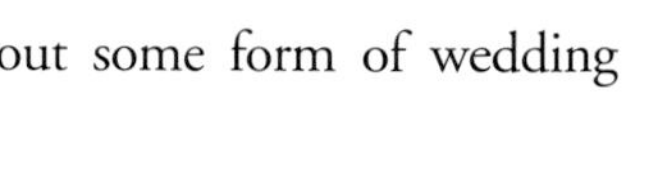

insurance. You wouldn't dream of driving a car without insurance, yet many couples are happy to risk anything up to £20,000 when it comes to their wedding. The average policy covers most eventualities and for under £100 is well worth the investment.

Your venue

The key questions

Q Is the venue you want available? Lots of popular venues get booked up well in advance so check early that it's likely to be free. Your venue shouldn't completely dictate your wedding date so be prepared to shop around.

Q Is it in the right location? If you are having a church wedding, the reception venue needs to be within about 20 minutes' drive. If it's a summer wedding, check out the use of outside areas and gardens.

Q Is it big enough – or perhaps too big? Your venue needs to be big enough to comfortably seat all your guests, with separate areas for drinks and dancing. If you are having a small wedding you don't want a venue with overly large rooms – it would feel as though half your guests hadn't turned up!

Q What does the venue look like? Take a good look at the decorative style of all the venues. Fixtures and fittings such as carpets, curtains and general décor can't be changed and will need to work with your chosen colour scheme or theme. Is it clean and tidy and in good decorative order?

Q Is this the right venue for your budget? The reception takes a big slice of the wedding budget so check exactly what is included in any hire charges and read the small print about what you are, and aren't, allowed to do.

Finding the perfect venue is one of your most important tasks, so arrange to view potential places when you have plenty of time and are clear about what you want. That means knowing the proposed wedding date, the number of expected guests, your budget and having a rough idea of the overall style you want.

Spend a little time on the venue's website before making any appointment to view. It will give you a lot of background information and may well answer many of your questions straight away, saving everyone time and effort.

Your main contacts will be the manager and the on-site events co-ordinator, if there is one. These are the people who'll show you around and answer all your questions about facilities and prices. Arm yourself with a list of what you need to know (see our Venue Suitability worksheet) and gauge how well the person answers the questions.

Do they seem willing to consider new ideas or does anything unusual just seem like too much trouble? Their overall attitude will speak volumes about how much effort they will put into your wedding. You want to develop a rapport with them and feel they share your vision.

Ask who will be your main contact as the plans progress and whether they'll be assigned to your wedding all the way through. You need the reassurance that the person who has been involved in all your plans will be around to ensure the smooth running of your big day from the minute your guests arrive to when the last one leaves.

Venue suitability

These are things you will need to know in your search for the perfect wedding venue.

Name of venue

- Website
- Contact name
- Telephone number
- E-mail
- Available date(s)

- ❑ Does the venue have a civil licence?
- ❑ Does it have an on-site wedding co-ordinator?
- ❑ Is there a location hire fee?
- ❑ Does it have on-site catering?
- ❑ Can we bring our own alcohol?
- ❑ Is there a corkage charge?
- ❑ What is the package price per head?
- ❑ Are tables, chairs, linens and tableware included?
- ❑ Will there be other events on the same day?
- ❑ Is there overnight accommodation?
- ❑ Are room discounts available for guests?
- ❑ Is there adequate parking for guests?
- ❑ Can we put up a marquee?
- ❑ Can we use the venue gardens?
- ❑ Is the venue insured in case of accident?
- ❑ Will the reception have to end at a certain time?
- ❑ Can we let off fireworks?
- ❑ Are small children welcome?
- ❑ Is there a cancellation policy?
- ❑ What is the estimated cost of using the venue?

Name of venue

Website

Contact name

Telephone number

E-mail

Available date(s)

- ❑ Does the venue have a civil licence?
- ❑ Does it have an on-site wedding co-ordinator?
- ❑ Is there a location hire fee?
- ❑ Does it have on-site catering?
- ❑ Can we bring our own alcohol?
- ❑ Is there a corkage charge?
- ❑ What is the package price per head?
- ❑ Are tables, chairs, linens and tableware included?
- ❑ Will there be other events on the same day?
- ❑ Is there overnight accommodation?
- ❑ Are room discounts available for guests?
- ❑ Is there adequate parking for guests?
- ❑ Can we put up a marquee?
- ❑ Can we use the venue gardens?
- ❑ Is the venue insured in case of accident?
- ❑ Will the reception have to end at a certain time?
- ❑ Can we let off fireworks?
- ❑ Are small children welcome?
- ❑ Is there a cancellation policy?
- ❑ What is the estimated cost of using the venue?

Your notes

Your wedding photographer

The key questions

Q Have you asked around for recommendations? **Do you know anyone who has been married recently or have you seen a wedding album that you like? Look at the real weddings section on www.youandyourwedding.co.uk for inspiration or contact a professional association such as the Master Photographer's Association.**

Q Do you want a certain style? **How do you see your wedding photographs? Romantic or modern? Colour or black and white? Check whether a potential photographer specialises in one particular look or whether they work with various different styles.**

Q How much of the day do you want photographed? **Do you want photographs of every part of the day or just the ceremony and important moments such as cutting the cake? How much does the price drop if the photographer is there for only part of the day?**

Q What is your budget? **Prices vary enormously and you'll need to do your homework, comparing what's on offer to find the best photographer. It is important that you like him or her too!**

Popular wedding photographers get booked up quickly, so start looking as soon as possible. Decide on the style of photos you prefer. Do you want traditional shots or a more relaxed, reportage style? Choose someone who specialises in your preferred look. Reportage photography may look easy but it takes a certain skill to capture 'unposed' moments well.

You should always ask to see a few previous wedding albums, not just a carefully compiled portfolio of the best shots from several weddings. You want to make sure the standard is consistent throughout the whole day.

A question of copyright

Many couples are surprised that they don't own the copyright to the pictures after the wedding, which means you don't get the negatives or images on disk and have to pay for each print made. This should all be clear in the initial agreement, including the number of prints in the package price.

The videographer

If you'd like a wedding video, the videographer may well work at the same studio as the photographer. Or your photographer can probably recommend someone they have worked with before. It's important that the two of them have a good rapport since you don't want them getting in each other's way.

Ask to see samples of the videographer's work. Again, you want to see a complete video, not carefully edited highlights from several weddings. You are paying as much for the post-production as the footage that is shot on the day. The addition of music, special effects such as slow motion, and captions can make your video look more like a feature film than a home movie.

Styles of wedding photography

Romantic: Every bride will want a few traditional and shamelessly romantic shots.
Reportage: Relaxed, informal shots that create a storybook feel.
Black and white: Even if you love colour pictures, it's still a good idea to include a few stylish black and white shots.
Sepia: Instantly recognisable brownish or blueish shots, reminiscent of very early photographic styles, that can be especially flattering.
Hand tinting: This is a special technique where the photographer adds splashes of colour to black and white prints.
Digital images: Many photographers use a digital camera, which means computer wizardry can be used to remove blemishes, eliminate 'red eye' and even change the colour of the sky.

Finding a photographer

You should aim to see two or three photographers and their work before making your final choice.

Name of photographer/studio

Primary contact

Date of phone call

Contact number

Address

E-mail

Website

References

Meeting date

Package price(s)

Your notes

Name of photographer/studio

Primary contact

Date of phone call

Contact number

Address

E-mail

Website

References

Meeting date

Package price(s)

Your notes

Your Suppliers

Your Reception

Dressed to Thrill

Your Wedding Gifts

Your Honeymoon

One Week and Counting

Photography checklist

Give a copy of this to the photographer and a second copy to a trusted friend, such as the best man, to ensure all the shots you want are taken.

With the bride/groom prior to the wedding

❑ The bride and her maids getting ready
❑ The wedding dress and accessories
❑ The bridal bouquet
❑ The bride's mother and the bridesmaids leaving for the ceremony
❑ The bride and her father leaving for the ceremony
❑ The groom and best man getting ready

Before/during the ceremony

❑ The groom and best man outside the ceremony
❑ The wedding rings on a cushion or prayer book
❑ The wedding transport
❑ The bride arriving at the ceremony
❑ The bride walking down the aisle
❑ The ceremony
❑ Signing the register
❑ The first married kiss

After the ceremony

❑ The bride and groom
❑ The bride and groom and their families outside the ceremony
❑ The couple and the main bridal party
❑ The bride and her parents
❑ The groom and his parents
❑ The couple and both sets of parents
❑ The couple and their respective work colleagues
❑ The couple with all their guests (if room allows)

The reception

- ❑ The reception venue before the guests arrive
- ❑ Close-up details of the tables
- ❑ Close-up details like favours, menu cards and so on
- ❑ The wedding cake
- ❑ The entrance of the bride and groom to the reception
- ❑ Guests at the top table
- ❑ The speeches
- ❑ The toast
- ❑ The couple cutting the cake
- ❑ The first dance as man and wife
- ❑ Bride dancing with her father
- ❑ Bride tossing her bouquet
- ❑ The couple leaving at the end of the reception

Your notes

Your Suppliers

Your Reception

Dressed to Thrill

Your Wedding Gifts

Your Honeymoon

One Week and Counting

Your florist

The key questions

Q Do they seem creative? **You need to find someone who shares your vision for your wedding. Arm yourself with pictures from magazines and expect to be inspired.**

Q What time of year are you marrying? **Although just about any flower is available all year round – at a price – using seasonal flowers for your wedding will look right and save you money. Find out from your florist what will be available and in what colours.**

Q How many flowers do you want, and where? **Be clear from the outset about how many floral arrangements you want and where you want them to go. Do you need a lot of flowers at the ceremony? Most time is spent at the reception, so this is where the majority of the flower budget should be spent.**

Q How much of your budget is set aside for flowers? **It's essential to find a florist who can come up with good ideas to suit how much you have to spend. If they keep trying to get you to spend more than you've allocated, this florist is not the one for you.**

Aromatic wedding flowers

Create a fragrant memory for your guests by choosing wedding flowers with beautiful and distinctive scents.

Freesia	Jasmine	Magnolia
Gardenia	Lilac	Rose
Hyacinth	Lily	Stephanotis
Iris	Lily of the valley	Sweet pea

Q What flowers do you like? **Make a list of your favourite flowers. If the blooms you would like are particularly expensive, remember that just a few can make an impact if used creatively.**

The secret behind the best wedding flowers is finding the right florist. Start your search six to nine months before the wedding and expect to finalise all the details about three weeks before the big day.

Questions to ask your florist:

- Do you have photographs of your work?
- Have you worked at my venues before?
- What type of flowers will be available when I am getting married?
- What are the latest trends? Is colour in or out? What are the most popular types of bouquet?
- Should I choose a colour theme for the whole day?
- Are you a member of any professional associations?
- What shape of bouquet will work with the style of my dress (take along a shot of your gown and a fabric swatch if possible)?
- Given my budget, what type of centrepieces do you recommend?
- How will the ceremony and reception flowers co-ordinate?
- What happens if the flowers I ordered are unavailable on the day?
- Will you be doing the flowers for my wedding? If not, can I meet the florist(s) who will be?
- Can flowers be moved from the ceremony to the reception?
- Can you provide vases, napkin holders, candelabra and so on? What will they cost? Will you arrange collection of these after the wedding?
- Are there any other costs beyond flowers, vases, labour and delivery?
- Do I have to pay a deposit? When is the balance due to be paid?
- What is your cancellation policy?

What flowers do you need?

Make a list of all the areas in your wedding where you would like to include flowers. Try to visualise the ceremony room, the reception venue, your bouquet, your bridesmaids' flowers, buttonholes and any other accessories.

Wedding flowers you may like to include:

- a welcome garland outside the ceremony venue
- a pedestal arrangement at the altar or on the registrar's table at a civil wedding
- pew end or chair back decorations
- cones of fresh petals to use as confetti
- centrepieces for each reception table
- flowers to top the cake and decorate the cake table
- individual flowers to adorn each napkin
- the bride's bouquet
- posies for the bridesmaids
- buttonholes and corsages for the main bridal party
- thank-you bouquets for each mother and any other special guests
- flower arrangements in each of the venue toilets

Flowers on a budget

Flowers are expensive and if your budget is tight you'll have to be creative about what you choose. Find out if there's another wedding at the church on the same day and ask if you can share the flowers with the other couple(s), and think about moving the ceremony arrangements to decorate an area at the reception. The good news is that less is often more and it really isn't necessary to cover every surface with flowers. A few carefully placed, eye-catching arrangements can do the job just as well as elaborate centrepieces on every table.

One good tip is to choose seasonal flowers, since they will offer the best value for money, and ask your florist about incorporating foliage or using striking vases and containers that will draw the eye. Think about using well-loved flowers such as carnations, daffodils and tulips rather than the traditional and more expensive wedding favourites. In the hands of a skilled florist they'll look amazing in generous bunches in large vases.

Be inventive with your centrepieces and consider ideas such as floating flower heads or petals in bowls of water, using tall vases of citrus fruits topped with one layer of complementary flowers, or putting a row of flowering plants into brightly coloured pots and lining them up along each table – these can double up as favours for your guests to take home after the wedding.

Styles of bridal bouquet

The bride's bouquet is the ultimate wedding accessory and you'll want to work with your florist to create something extra special.

Hand-tied: Blooms, usually a variety of roses, wired together or casually hand-tied. They work best at a contemporary wedding with a simple, modern dress.
Pomander: A tight ball of flowers, usually without foliage, suspended on a ribbon that the bride hangs on her wrist. These are also very popular for bridesmaids of all ages.
Posy: Small, simple and usually hand-tied with ribbon. Lily of the valley makes the perfect minimalist posy.
Round: The classic bouquet, usually consisting of larger flowers such as roses and peonies loosely arranged and tied with ribbon.
Shower: A waterfall-like spill of flowers wired to cascade from a handle. This is the most traditional and formal of the bouquet shapes and suits full-skirted dresses.

Flowers for all seasons

Spring flowers

Amaryllis: A large open flower in pure white to brightest red. Perfect for larger bouquets and centrepieces.

Anemone: Available in 120 different varieties. The brighter colours are great for trendy posies.

Daffodil: A bright yellow flower, always popular for spring weddings.

Freesia: Small, highly scented flowers in bright colours. Ideal for headdresses and posies.

Gerbera: Large and dramatic daisy-like flowers in many bright colours.

Lily of the valley: Tiny bell-shaped white flowers with a sweet fragrance. A classic wedding flower and ideal for small posies. Expensive.

Orchid: Exotic and pricey but available in a variety of pretty colours. Just a few long stems simply tied make a stunning modern bouquet.

Ranunculus: A buttercup-shaped flower popular for spring weddings. Available in a variety of colours.

Stephanotis: A traditional and popular small white wedding flower with a wonderful sweet scent.

Sweet pea: A classic wedding favourite with delicate petals and a sweet, lingering fragrance.

Summer flowers

Anthurium: Famous for its glossy, waxy-looking flowers. Popular for beach and tropical themes.

Carnation: The traditional choice for a buttonhole and available in lots of colours. Also works well en masse in pomanders for bridesmaids.

Chrysanthemum: A versatile flower ranging from daisy-like flowers to large pom-pom shapes.

Gypsophila: Tiny white or pink flowers that form a cloud-like display. Best used in quantity.

Lily: There are about a hundred varieties in a huge range of colours. Particularly good for centrepieces.

Magnolia: Large, subtly scented flowers in a wide range of shapes and colours. Popular for reception decoration.

Peony: Large, fragrant flowers with petals in a bowl shape. A popular bouquet flower in shades of pink or white.

Rose: The most popular of all the wedding flowers and used for bouquets and decorations. Available in a huge variety of sizes, varieties and colours and many are scented.

Sunflower: A refreshing choice for a summer wedding. They can be pricey but are so big you don't need many to make a visual impact.

Autumn flowers

Agapanthus: Large, bell-shaped flowers in a striking shade of violet. They add a splash of colour to bouquets and centrepieces.

Aster: A small, daisy-like flower in a wide variety of colours, usually with a bright yellow centre. Pretty in bouquets.

Clematis: Perfect for trailing bouquets. Available in a good selection of sizes and colours.

Daisy: An all-year-round favourite that always looks bright and cheerful. An ideal flower on which to theme your whole wedding.

Hosta: Not strictly a flower but a popular variety of foliage often used in wedding bouquets. Its heart-shaped leaves range in colour from soft to brilliant green.

Hydrangea: Large, full flowers in a variety of pretty pastel colours. Good for centrepieces and pedestal arrangements.

Passion flower: A large, exotic flower that can be used to add splashes of bright colour.

Pinks: Not surprisingly, available in a variety of shades of pink – from very pale to almost red. Pretty round flowers that are ideal for bouquets.

Winter flowers

Camellia: Beautiful open-faced flowers ranging from a single row of petals to overlapping multi-rows. Popular for buttonholes because of their richly coloured foliage.

Euphorbia: An evergreen shrub with yellowish flowers. Useful as an all-year-round addition to venue arrangements and more elaborate bouquets.
Iris: An unusual fan-shaped flower with three large petals. Usually lilac, purple or white and popular for centrepieces.
Nerine: Sprays of hot or pale pink trumpet-shaped flowers. Fairly exotic, so good for more unusual centrepieces.
Pansy: Small, flat-faced flowers in a variety of colours and intensities. Can be kept in a pot to double up as a table decoration and pretty favour.
Snowdrop: A delicate white flower and one of the classic bridal blooms. Ideal in hand-tied posies and for smaller table decorations.
Tulip: A cheerful favourite available in a wide range of colours. The varieties with frilled edges are very popular for contemporary bouquets.

The meaning of flowers

Send a secret message of love to your groom with the flowers you choose for your bouquet.

Flower	Meaning
Azalea	True to the end
Camellia	Perfect love
Carnation (red)	Admiration
Carnation (white)	Sweet and lovely
Daffodil	Joy
Gardenia	Purity and joy
Iris	Hope and wisdom
Jasmine	Sensuality
Lemon blossom	Fidelity
Lily of the valley	Happiness
Rose (red)	I love you
Stephanotis	Marital happiness
Tulip (red)	Love
Tulip (yellow)	Sunshine of my life
Violet	Faithfulness

Wedding flower planner

It will help to note down the styles, colours and types of flowers for each part of the wedding day.

	Flowers/colours	Quantity	Cost
Personal flowers			£
Bridal bouquet			£
Bridesmaids' bouquets			£
Flower girl basket			£
Groom's buttonhole			£
Ushers' buttonholes			£
Mothers' corsages			£
Fathers' buttonholes			£
Ceremony flowers			£
Altar			£
Pews			£
Aisle			£
Window ledges			£
Entrance			£
Other			£
Reception flowers			£
Top table			£
Centrepieces for each table			£
Chair backs			£
Napkins			£
Buffet table			£
Cake top			£
Cake table			£
Guest book table			£
Entrance			£
Other			£

	Flowers/colours	Quantity	Cost
Miscellaneous flowers			£
Vases			£
Candelabra			£
Fireplace garlands			£
Flowers for toilets			£
Thank-you bouquets			
• Bride's mother			£
• Groom's mother			£
• Other			£
Potted plants			£
Other			£
Other			£
Other			£
Total flower budget			£

Your notes

Your wedding stationery

The key questions

Q Which stationery will reflect your wedding style? **The invitations are the first indication your guests will have of the overall style of the day. The more formal the wedding, the more traditional the invitation should be. You can choose from everything from a classic card to a quirky note. E-mailed invitations are not polite, so don't go there.**

Q How should the invitations be worded and presented? **First and foremost, the invitation has a job to do – clearly and simply telling guests the when, where and how of your wedding. Incorporate your colour scheme into the invitations somewhere, perhaps a ribbon trim or a coloured insert inside each envelope.**

Q What other stationery do you need? **You'll also need to think about whether you want 'save the date' cards, RSVP cards, an order of service, a table plan, name cards, menus – even match books. These are best ordered from the same supplier so everything looks co-ordinated and has the same design.**

Q What is your budget? **You can order wedding stationery from many different sources – specialist wedding stationery companies, high street stationers, department stores and the internet – if you are good with a computer package, you could always save money and make your own at home.**

You should ideally choose your stationery about six months before the big day, allowing plenty of time to organise quantities, printing, delivery, addressing envelopes and then sending them about 12 weeks before the wedding.

Who receives an invitation?

- one invitation per couple
- one invitation for each of your attendants and their partners
- one invitation for the officiant and his/her wife/husband
- one invitation per single guest
- each child over 18 usually gets an individual invitation, even if he or she will be coming with their parents; younger children are named on their parent's invitation
- 20+ spare invitations for additional guests and to keep as mementos
- 30+ spare envelopes to allow for additional guests and mistakes

Invitation wording

The hosts of the wedding traditionally send out the invitations; this is often the bride's parents but it could also be the groom's parents or, more likely these days, the couple themselves. If you already have children or it is a second marriage and either of you has children, it's a nice touch to send the invitations from the children.

If you are not sure what to say, ask your stationer for advice – they'll know all the options – and feel free to adapt traditional wording to suit your family circumstances and the formality of the wedding.

Don't forget to put the name of the person who will be handling the RSVPs, including a daytime telephone number, and a date by when you would ideally like to receive a reply on the invitation. RSVPs are usually handled by the chief bridesmaid, the mother or sister of the bride, or a trusted and well-organised friend.

It is usual to leave a space within the invitation to write in the guests' names or to write their names in the top right hand corner.

Bride's parents as church wedding hosts

Mr and Mrs Robert Jones
request the pleasure of your company
at the marriage of their daughter
Deborah Jane
to
James Smith
3.00pm, Saturday 20th October 2007
at St Paul's Church, Amersham
and afterwards for dinner and dancing at
Danesfield House, Marlow, Buckinghamshire
RSVP to Mrs Robert Jones [insert telephone number] by 22nd September

Couple hosting their own civil ceremony

Ms Deborah Jane Jones
and
Mr James Smith
request the pleasure of your company
at their marriage
3.00pm, Saturday 20th October 2007
at Danesfield House, Marlow, Buckinghamshire
The civil ceremony will be followed by
dinner and dancing at 5.00pm
RSVP to Suzanne Jones [inset telephone number] by 22nd September

Evening-only invitation

Deborah Jones and James Smith
request the pleasure of your company
following their marriage on 20th October 2007.
Please join us at 8.00pm for cake and dancing
at Danesfield House, Marlow, Buckinghamshire
RSVP to Suzanne Jones [insert telephone number] by 22nd September

Single or widowed parent hosting the wedding

Mr Robert Jones
requests the pleasure of your company
at the marriage of his daughter
Deborah Jane
to
James Smith
at St Paul's Church, Amersham
3.00pm, Saturday 20th October 2007
and afterwards for dinner and dancing at
Danesfield House, Marlow, Buckinghamshire
RSVP to Suzanne Jones [insert telephone number] by 22nd September

Divorced parents hosting the wedding

Mr Robert Jones and Mrs Emma Jones
request the pleasure of your company
at the marriage of their daughter
Deborah Jane
to
James Smith
3.00pm, Saturday 20th October 2007
at Danesfield House, Marlow, Buckinghamshire
The civil ceremony will be followed by
dinner and dancing at 5.00pm
RSVP to Suzanne Jones [insert telephone number]
by 22nd September

Children inviting (and for a second marriage)

Jessica and Finlay
invite you to celebrate the marriage
of their parents
Deborah Jones and James Smith
at 3.00pm, Saturday 20th October 2007
at Danesfield House, Marlow, Buckinghamshire
The civil ceremony will be followed by
dinner and dancing at 5.00pm
RSVP to Suzanne Jones (insert telephone number) by 22nd September

RSVP cards

The safest way to guarantee a quick response is to enclose an RSVP card and envelope with the invitation. It needs simple wording and a response date (about three or four weeks before the wedding) in the bottom right corner.

.... *are delighted to accept/unfortunately have to decline your kind wedding invitation.*

Printing techniques

Calligraphy: Formal script handwriting, done by hand. Expensive.
Embossed: Raised lettering or decoration, usually used for style details. Also an expensive option.
Engraving: Lettering done using a copperplate die to 'cut' the letters into the paper. The letters feel raised on the front and back of the paper.
Letterpress: Similar to but slightly cheaper than engraving. It impresses words into the paper.
Offset: The most popular and cost-effective method of printing. It uses a rubber cylinder to transfer inked letters on to the paper.
Overlays: A decorative idea where translucent paper is put on top of a printed invitation and the two are tied together, usually with ribbon.

Wedding stationery

Note down the essential details to ensure nothing gets forgotten from your stationery order.

Name of stationery supplier

Contact name

Telephone number

E-mail

Website

Items required	Quantity	Price
Save the date cards		£
Invitations		£
Envelopes		£
RSVP cards		£
Envelopes		£
Directions/map		£
Gift list details		£
Table plan		£
Order of service		£
Place cards		£
Table numbers		£
Menu		£
Other		£
Postage		£
Calligraphy		£
Total stationery budget		£

Deposit due date

Balance due date

Order delivery date

Wedding transport

The key questions

Q Do you need special cars? It's usual to provide transport for the bride and her father and the mother of the bride and the bridesmaids. This not only allows you to arrive in style but will also look good in your photographs. But if you have a friend with a large car who doesn't mind driving, this is perfectly acceptable.

Q What distances are involved? Hopefully you won't have to travel far between your home, the ceremony and the reception. If driving more than a few miles is necessary, you'll have to forget anything like a horse and carriage and most vintage cars since they can be booked for only short journeys. If guests need to travel between the ceremony and the venue, you could lay on transport to save them using their own cars; Routemaster buses are the latest trend! It is the best man's duty to make sure that all the guests have transport from the church to the reception.

Q What style of transport would you like? If you are having a themed wedding or just want a great-looking car to show off in your photographs, splashing out on wedding transport could be money well spent. There is masses of choice, from the traditional Rolls Royce to stretch limos, available in an assortment of colours, and even helicopters and hot air balloons for the most dramatic entrances and exits.

Q How much does your budget allow? **Shop around for good deals. You can sometimes get a special rate if you book several cars from the same company. Don't dismiss your local cab company either – you don't necessarily have to use a specialist wedding firm. It's a good idea to see the actual cars you'll have on the day and to make it clear that they must be spotless inside.**

There are lots of specialist car hire companies providing everything from super-modern to vintage cars that will bring a stylish touch to the day. Just make sure any car you use can accommodate your dress without crushing the fabric too much; you don't want to arrive in a crumpled mess.

When you book your car, ask whether the company charges by the hour or per job so you can work out how much it will cost to have them collect you from home, take you to the venue and on to the reception. The bride and groom usually provide a car for the mother of the bride and the bridesmaids as well, in which case you may be offered a better rate for booking two or more cars at the same time.

Your groom might like to splash out on hiring himself a sports car to take him and his best man to the ceremony. It won't come cheap, but he'll love having the chance to drive a Ferrari or an E-type Jaguar for the day – and of course, you get to travel in it too if you are leaving the reception and going off to your first night hotel. Even if drink doesn't permit this, you can always use the car as a stylish backdrop for some of your wedding photographs.

One final word on transport: make sure your venue has sufficient parking for all your guests. If not, include details of local car parks and local parking restrictions with the invitations.

Wedding transport

Everything you need to think about to ensure you all get to the church on time!

	Pickup time/location	Transport	Cost
To the ceremony			
Bride and father			£
Bride's mother			£
Bridesmaids			£
Groom			£
Best man			£
Ushers			£
Groom's parents			£
To the reception			
Bride and groom			£
Bride's parents			£
Groom's parents			£
Bridesmaids			£
Best man			£
Ushers			£
Other guests			£
After the reception			
Bride and groom			£
Bride's parents			£
Groom's parents			£
Bridesmaids			£
Best man			£
Ushers			£
Other guests			£
Total budget			£

Musicians and entertainers

The key questions

Q What do you need? Think about important moments during your day. At the ceremony, do you want an organist/a string quartet/a choir? Do you want music while your guests are eating? And, if the wedding includes evening entertainment, will you need to book a band or a DJ, as well as other styles of entertainment such as a magician or a caricature artist?

Q How can you set the right mood? Choose the musical style according to the formality of the wedding. A grand venue and formal meal will be best accompanied by a live band. A funky DJ is more in keeping with a civil ceremony and cocktails. If the rooms are large, remember to check whether speakers will be necessary – and if they are permitted.

Q How can all tastes be catered for? Your guests are bound to be a mixture of ages and they won't all share the same taste in music. You'll find choosing a mixture of classics and modern songs will appeal to most people. If you want the dance floor heaving, 70s and 80s disco tunes are always popular.

Q What is your budget? The more performers you have the greater the cost so, if your budget is limited, think about keeping things simple: have just an organist for the ceremony; compile a CD of your favourite background music to play during the meal; and then book a DJ for the evening.

Ask your friends for recommendations for musicians or entertainers they know so you can narrow down a shortlist. Once you've done that, it's important that you hear them play, live if possible, and don't rely on someone else's opinion. You want to aim for music that will suit the taste of the majority of your guests so a middle-of-the-road route is usually your best option. There's nothing worse than an empty dance floor or your older relatives wanting to leave early because they are being deafened by a rock band, and your younger friends won't expect anything too cutting edge.

Check with the officiant and the venue about any restrictions on numbers and noise levels before you book anyone for the ceremony and the reception. Let performers know how many guests are coming and where and for how long you want them to play. Most wedding bands and DJs have a play list so make sure you look through this and delete any songs you detest.

You may want to think about other ways to entertain your guests at the reception. There are lots of magicians, mime artists and caricaturists who can walk around entertaining each table. It all depends on the amount of entertainment you want to offer your guests and, of course, your budget.

Do you want to dance?

There's few things worse than an empty dance floor so make sure your DJ includes a selection of favourites and you can't go wrong.

- Abba
- The Beatles
- The Bee Gees
- Earth, Wind and Fire
- The Fatback Band
- Gloria Gaynor
- Michael Jackson
- Kylie
- Madonna
- The Police
- The Rolling Stones
- The Scissor Sisters
- Sister Sledge
- UB40
- Village People
- Barry White
- Robbie Williams
- Stevie Wonder

Music and entertainment

From ceremony to reception, everything you need to think about for entertaining your guests.

	Name	Contact details
Ceremony		
Organist		
Choir		
Soloist		
String quartet		
Other		
Estimated cost		

Your notes

	Name	Contact details
Reception		
Band		
Rentals/equipment		
DJ		
Magician		
Children's entertainer		
Crèche		
Fireworks		
Other		
Estimated cost		

Your notes

The wedding planner

The key questions

Q Do you need a wedding planner? **If you have a particularly hectic job or are planning a long-distance wedding, a wedding planner could be invaluable, saving you time, money and definitely stress.**

Q What do wedding planners do? **Most offer two services. The simplest option is a pre-wedding consultation service helping to find a venue or suppliers and answering basic questions. Or you can involve them in every part of your wedding, planning every detail and being there on the day to ensure it all comes together and fulfils your dreams.**

Q Are they worth the money? **If you're not a natural organiser and the thought of dealing with suppliers, making decisions and handling deadlines is just not your thing – and you don't have a willing mother to help either – a wedding planner is a good bet. They will have great contacts and can save you money by negotiating the best deals.**

Q What will it cost? **The cost of a wedding planner varies enormously but expect to pay either a set fee for a set number of tasks undertaken, or a percentage fee of the total budget.**

You may need a wedding planner if:

- your wedding venue is some distance from your home or is abroad
- you have a high-pressure job and not enough time
- you are easily daunted by the thought of planning a family party, let alone a wedding
- you are having arguments with everyone already – it may be easier to get someone else to make the decisions
- you find negotiating prices with suppliers difficult or embarrassing
- you haven't a clue where to start – on anything at all!

Your Reception

Now it's time to plan your reception. Organising the biggest and best party of your life – not to mention the most expensive – takes time and effort if you want to be sure of giving your guests an occasion to remember.

The key questions

Q When is the wedding? Many of the best wedding venues get booked up well in advance so you'll have to start your search early as competition will be hot! If you can possibly be flexible with the date, you'll probably find that even the most popular venue has availability on a weekday or a Sunday.

Q Where will it be? If you've chosen a church ceremony, the reception venue needs to be within about a 20-minute drive of the church if you don't want to risk your guests getting lost. If you are planning a civil ceremony, is the venue too far away from where most guests live so they will have to factor accommodation or expensive taxis into the equation? Do you want a venue that suits a summer or a winter wedding?

Q How many guests? Usually, the more people you invite, the more formal the wedding. Is the venue big enough – or too big, if you want a small, intimate party? Do you want a traditional sit-down meal and dancing or is a simple lunch party more your style? Do the maths; can you really afford a big wedding?

Q What atmosphere are you looking for? As you view any prospective venue, try to 'feel' the atmosphere. Does is feel stuffy and overly formal so your guests might be intimidated? How friendly are the staff?

Look at the room where you'll be eating, preferably at the same time of day you would be using it. Does it feel bright and welcoming? Will the colour scheme of the carpets and curtains suit your theme?

Q What is your budget? **The reception takes the biggest slice of the wedding budget – around 40 per cent – so you need to shop around and compare prices of everything from the venue to the catering, drinks and entertainment. Before signing on the dotted line for anything, ask yourselves if you could get a better deal elsewhere.**

The basics

Any reception has many different elements that all need to come together seamlessly and on time on the big day. As soon as you've set the date, start thinking about the following:

Caterers: You'll need to decide whether to use the venue's caterer or an independent company. Get quotes from at least two caterers so you can compare prices and expect to book someone at least six to nine months before the wedding.

Your menu: Your wedding isn't the time to experiment with clever food that may not be to everyone's taste. Try to take a middle ground and taste all suggested dishes before making your final choices about four to six months before the wedding.

Your cake: Your caterers may have a suitable on-staff baker or you may want to look for a specialist cake maker. Aim to make your final decision four to six months before the wedding.

Drinks: Work with the venue and your caterers over the drinks selection once the menu has been finalised. Think about having a cocktail reception to welcome your guests to the reception. Drink decisions should be made four to six months before the wedding.

Décor: The venue may be supplying tables and chairs or you may need to hire them. Work with the venue, caterers and florist over colour schemes and set-up details, finalising choices three to six months before the wedding.

Guest list: You'll be expected to finalise numbers one or two weeks before the wedding and supply a table plan so the room can be arranged.

You'll need to reconfirm all the main details, timings, contact names and numbers with all suppliers a week before the wedding. Do this in writing, followed by a phone call to double check that everything is under control.

Your caterers and menu

The key questions

Q What are the catering options? **Depending on the venue you choose you can either use the on-site caterers, which is normal at hotels and banqueting rooms, or bring your own caterers to the venue. Whichever type of catering you choose, you'll most likely be offered a 'per head' price – set menu options for a set price. This may or may not include a set number of drinks and things such as linen and glasses hire; it all depends on the type of contract on offer so always check the small print.**

Q Should you have a sit-down meal or a buffet? **If you want a formal wedding with a meal followed by dancing, most people have a sit-down meal with waiting staff. A buffet is more suited to an informal reception where you want to create a relaxed atmosphere. Speak to your caterers about the type of event you want and see what they suggest. It may be that you have waiter service for the starter and desserts and a buffet choice of meat and fish dishes for the main course.**

Q Do you have to give your guests food? **There is nothing to say you have to feed your guests a full meal. There is now a trend towards receptions with cocktails and substantial canapés, with an informal atmosphere and lasting only a couple of hours. This is certainly a stylish option if money is limited – much better than serving a budget sit-down meal – but do make sure you make it clear on the invitations so that people don't come expecting a traditional reception and dancing into the night.**

Q How do you plan a good menu? **Planning a menu is a skilled task if you want to please the taste buds of the majority of your guests and yet still look as though you've used some imagination. Work with your caterers to come up with a balanced menu of seasonal ideas and always taste all suggested dishes before agreeing to anything.**

Choosing your caterers

The food you serve your guests can make or break your reception so you'll want the best caterers to make sure everything is first class. There are two main options: the in-house caterer based at your venue; and the off-site catering company, which brings everything to your venue.

Wedding packages are available at many venues, ranging in price depending on the style and formality of the event and the meals themselves. Generally speaking, the more formal the occasion, the more the catering is going to cost. Most packages include the food, the people to cook and serve it, the tables, chairs, linens, china, cutlery, glasses and bar staff, all priced on a 'per head' basis. Or if you want to use items outside the usual package – such as coloured linens, specific glasses or having chair covers – you can list everything you want and have it priced individually.

Depending on the venue, you may not have to use its in-house catering facilities. But if you particularly want to bring in someone of your own, you are likely to be charged a lot for the privilege and it may be more cost effective and a lot less hassle to look for a different venue.

If the reception venue is unfurnished, such as a marquee or the village hall, you'll probably use a mixture of hire companies and outside caterers. The room will be a blank space so you'll need to hire everything from tables and chairs to the glasses. Some catering companies can help with all of this, others provide just food.

Once you've chosen a caterer, ask for a tasting session of the proposed menu and drink options. Discuss the menu, canapés, guest numbers, vegetarian and special dietary options and when you need to confirm and pay for everything. Don't be afraid to make changes to their food suggestions; it's your wedding and you need to love, not just like, what you'll be serving to your friends and family. Caterers are professionals and won't be at all offended if you want something different.

At the same time as finalising the menu you should choose appropriate wines to complement your carefully chosen menu.

Reception dos and don'ts

Do welcome your guests with a drink and nibbles.
Don't keep them hanging around for ages while you have umpteen photographs taken.
Do have a receiving line if you want to say hello to all your guests.
Don't forget soft drinks, particularly during hot weather.
Do think about providing some kind of entertainment if you have a lot of guests under ten years old – their parents will love you for it!
Don't keep guests in the dark about timings. On arrival, everyone should know what time the meal will start and basics like whether they can smoke and where to find the toilets.
Do think about having a toastmaster to make announcements and keep things running smoothly.
Don't let the groom and best man have too much to drink before making their speeches.
Do have a seating plan so everyone knows where to sit.
Don't seat people together who have nothing in common.
Do practise your first dance beforehand.
Don't forget to tell your guests if you won't be leaving and intend to party until dawn.

Your wedding menu

So what food should you serve? The food is one of the most memorable parts of any wedding reception and will be long remembered by your guests, hopefully for all the right reasons! Work with your caterers to come up with an interesting, though not too adventurous, range of dishes that will suit most tastes from young to old.

Think about the time of day you are holding your reception before deciding on the style and formality of the food. Traditionally, the earlier in the day the celebration, the less formal it can be.

Brunch: Served from late morning to about 2pm and usually including a traditional breakfast such as scrambled eggs, smoked salmon, pastries, fruit and cheeses. This is followed by wedding cake and a champagne toast.

Lunch: A lighter menu and fewer courses than dinner, served between noon and 3pm. It can be a buffet or a more formal sit-down.

Afternoon tea: Sandwiches and cakes (including the wedding cake) served between 2pm and 5pm. It is usually accompanied by a champagne toast.

Cocktail party: Served between 4pm and 7pm and including a mixture of hot and cold canapés – either passed round by waiters or placed on tables around the room – and cocktails, followed by wedding cake and a champagne toast.

Dinner: Served between 5pm and 9pm and usually comprising three or four courses with wines, followed by wedding cake and a champagne toast. The food can be a buffet or served plated by waiting staff. The most formal option is for waiting staff to serve each guest from platters at the table.

Reception drinks

Apart from the food, alcoholic drinks are the other big part of the reception budget. You can buy your drinks direct from the venue or catering company, or buy from the local off-licence or supermarket and take it with you.

If you are thinking of providing your own drinks, be warned that most venues will charge you a corkage fee (anything up to £10 a bottle) to cover the cost of chilling, uncorking, pouring and serving it to your guests. Your cost-effective wine may not be such a bargain after all!

Champagne

Champagne is *the* wedding tipple and your guests will all want to indulge in at least one glass, even if it's just to toast the bride and groom. To be called champagne, the wine has to come from the Champagne region of France but there are lots of reasonably priced, and excellent, sparkling wines you may like to think about serving if bubbles are an important part of your celebrations. Try Spanish Cava or Italian Prosecco – both delicious and much more affordable.

Ask your caterer or local off-licence for recommendations and spend a weekend or two indulging in a tasting session. Brut on the label means it's dry, demi-sec is sweeter, and sec is the sweetest. Pink champagne is perfect for weddings and comes in a variety of colours from the palest pastel to a deep rose. Serve well chilled in tall flutes to maximise the bubbles.

Wine and cocktails

Cocktail parties are currently very much in vogue and are a stylish way to welcome guests to your reception. Ask the bartender at your venue to come up with two or three alternatives using the classic gin, vodka and non-alcoholic mixes and then you can give each one a name, personal to you or the wedding. Just keep an eye on what you're being charged for each cocktail as they tend to be easily consumed and can be pricey. If budget is a big issue, a bowl of punch – with a name of course – is a cost-effective option.

Regardless of the menu, your guests will expect to be offered a choice of red or white wine with the meal. Find out from the venue what they can offer and do try the house wines – a quality venue won't recommend a poor house wine, so they often combine quality with good value for money.

Soft drinks

You need to spare a thought for your guests who don't drink and for those who may be driving. In summer months in particular, everyone will welcome a glass of something non-alcoholic at some point in the evening. Water and orange juice are the classic offerings but a bit dull. How about providing flavoured waters, home-made lemonade and interesting fruit cordials? You can serve them chilled from ice-filled jugs.

10 budget-stretching tips

1 Have a lunch rather than dinner: people tend to eat and drink less earlier in the day.
2 Get married on a Sunday: people will drink less because of getting up for work the next day.
3 Compare prices: chicken is cheaper than beef; salmon is cheaper than sea bass.
4 Cut out the first course if you're serving substantial canapés.
5 Cut out the dessert and serve the wedding cake as pudding.
6 Choose affordable house wines and don't serve liqueurs.
7 Serve fruit punch rather than cocktails.
8 Put jugs of iced water on each table rather than using bottled water.
9 Tell the waiters to refresh glasses only when asked.
10 Introduce a pay bar at some point in the evening once the meal is over.

How much drink do you need?

- Allow about one drink per person per hour (slightly more during the summer when people tend to drink more).
- One bottle of wine serves about six partially filled glasses.
- One bottle of champagne fills about eight half-glasses.
- A magnum is two bottles, a jeroboam is four bottles.
- Most venues will let you buy on a sale-or-return basis, which means you pay only for the bottles that get opened.

WEDDING WORKSHEET

Catering checklist

All you need to know and what you'll need to cover in your catering agreement.

- ❑ Main contact
- ❑ Contact details
- ❑ Wedding date
- ❑ Start and finish times
- ❑ List of named rooms to be hired
- ❑ Menu and listed courses, with alternatives if not available
- ❑ Vegetarian or special meals requirements
- ❑ Cocktail reception drinks
- ❑ Drinks with meal
- ❑ Bar arrangements (open bar, part-pay bar, full-pay bar)
- ❑ Style of service (all served, some courses self-service)
- ❑ Number of waiting staff
- ❑ Number of bar staff
- ❑ Agreed price 'per head'
- ❑ Payment plan (always pay with a credit card if possible)
- ❑ Deposit and refund policy
- ❑ Date for final payment
- ❑ VAT, gratuities
- ❑ Cost of any overtime
- ❑ Cancellation policy
- ❑ Insurance cover
- ❑ Other

Your notes

Your wedding cake

Whether you choose a simple tiered classic or a tower of individual cupcakes, you'll want your cake to be a centre of attention at the reception – and to taste as good as it looks!

It's a good idea to decide on the style of your cake at the same time as the food. Your caterer's team may include a baker, the venue may be able to recommend a favourite supplier, or you can find a specialist cake maker in wedding magazines, such as *You & Your Wedding*, and through the Yellow Pages. For the budget-conscious couple, don't dismiss the high street. Many department stores also offer well-priced wedding cakes that can be stacked and decorated with flowers, ribbons or a mini bride and groom.

If you commission a cake maker, look through their portfolio of previous work and ask to sample a selection of the cakes. No matter how good it looks, it must taste delicious. Questions to ask your baker include, is the price per cake or per slice? What is the delivery charge? Can a cake stand and knife be provided? Do we pay a deposit and when is final payment due?

The icing on the cake

Topping the cake is a nice touch and you could add one of the following:

- The plastic bride-and-groom figures of yesteryear – they are making a comeback!
- Clay figures modelled to look like you and your groom.
- Fresh flowers to match your bouquet.
- Sugar hearts, flowers or your initials.
- Two doves.
- A heart-shaped photo frame holding a picture of the two of you.

An average three-tier cake will serve up to 100 guests and bear in mind the more complicated the design, the more expensive the cake will be. If you need to feed a large number of guests your baker can provide extra slices to keep in the kitchen to serve once the main cake has been cut.

Cake styles

The traditional wedding cake is a rich fruit cake, rather like Christmas cake, with a marzipan layer before a coating of royal icing. Your baker may use fondant icing if you want a lot of decoration because it gives a nice smooth surface for moulded flowers and piped details. But not everyone likes fruit cake, and more people are choosing wedding cakes made from chocolate or flavoured sponge. You can also mix each tier so there's something to please everyone. If you want to follow the tradition of keeping the top tier for your first child's christening, it needs to be fruit cake since you can't freeze and keep sponge for very long.

Another option is to choose an exotically flavoured cake and serve it as dessert – which will also help your budget. Once the main course is over you'll need to hold the cake-cutting ceremony and then the cake can be sliced and served for pudding. With the addition of ice-cream, cream or a fruity sauce, chocolate cake in particular works perfectly.

American stack: A popular and modern choice where each tier of the cake sits directly on top of another with no pillars in between.
Croquembouche: A French dessert where cream-filled choux pastry profiteroles are piled into a tower and covered in a rich toffee or chocolate sauce and spun sugar.
Cupcakes: Individual fairy cakes, one for each guest, are piled into a tower on a tiered cake stand. It makes a wonderful centrepiece as long as you don't want a traditional cake-cutting ceremony.
Traditional tiers: This is the most formal style of cake where small pillars are set four square to support each tier.

The wedding cake

You want to choose a cake that looks amazing and has your guests' taste buds watering.

Checklist

Cake style

Traditional stacked (with pillars)

American stacked (no pillars)

Individual fairy cakes

Croquembouche

Filling

Traditional fruit

Chocolate

Sponge

Mixture of flavours

Extras

Cake knife

Cake toppers

Cakemaker's details

Name

Address

Telephone Mobile

Email

Cake ordered

Size ordered

Price Deposit

Delivery date

Your notes

The menu planner

What food and drink will you be serving your guests?

	Item choice	Cost
Canapés		£
Cocktails		£
Welcome drinks		£
Appetiser		£
White wine		£
Red wine		£
Main course		£
Vegetarian alternative		£
Vegetables		£
Salad(s)		£
White wine		£
Red wine		£
Dessert(s)		£
Cheese		£
Dessert wine		£
Wedding cake		£
Champagne toast		£
Bottled water		£
Other		£
Total food budget		£
Budget per guest		£

Reception decoration

The key questions

Q How much decorating does your venue need? It's important when you view any potential venue that you pay particular attention to the décor of the rooms. For example, if you have a modern wedding in mind, a country house with gilt fitments and patterned wallpaper probably isn't for you. If you already have a colour scheme in mind, carpets, curtains and general fittings will have to complement your theme, not fight with it. Most historical buildings won't allow you to move much of the furniture either. It may be much simpler to look for another venue.

Q Do you need to spend a lot? You don't want to spend too much of your precious budget on decoration; after all it's only for a few hours and will all be taken down at the end of the evening. What you need to achieve is a few 'wow!' details that will focus the attention of your guests in the reception room where they will spend most of their time. Nicely coloured co-ordinated tables, welcoming flower arrangements, an eye-catching cake table and perhaps something like a chocolate fountain or even an ice sculpture will all make an impact. Work with your venue manager and your florist to see what cost-effective ideas they can suggest.

Q Who does the work? Any decorations that involve flowers will come under the guidance of the florist. The table decorations should be carried out by the venue and/or catering team. If you want time-consuming, fiddly touches it may be that you designate a creative friend or two to help out on the wedding morning tying bows and sprinkling table confetti to ensure it all looks just the way you want it.

Decorating your reception venue

Your guests will spend the majority of the day at the reception venue so you'll want to spend most of your decorating budget on making the room look good. How much you'll have to do will depend on the style of the venue.

- Less is usually more so keep it tasteful and don't get carried away covering every surface with (expensive) flowers, balloons, petals and bows.
- The same goes for a colour scheme; accents of colour looks stylish – but a pink tablecloth, pink napkins and pink chair covers don't!
- If the flower budget is tight, speak to your florist about creating one or two large, eye-catching arrangements to put near the entrance or on each side of the top table. You can then forget the individual table centrepieces.
- The latest trend is to have long rather than the traditional round tables. This looks very striking when the tables are laid end-to-end down the centre of a room, and conversation is often easier.
- If the choice of linens and glasses at the venue is limited or very plain, think about hiring a few striking details like coloured glasses or oversized coloured chargers.
- Plain or scruffy chairs can be transformed with chair covers, which come in a variety of colours and fabrics.

Seating your guests

Compiling the seating plan may sound easy, but in fact it can cause couples many headaches before they come up with the final arrangement. You'll need to think about dysfunctional families, groups of people who don't know one another, different age ranges and people you know won't get along. The seating plan is a juggling act of sometimes huge proportions and much

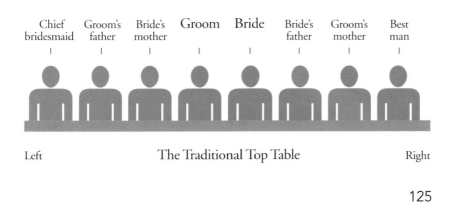

The Traditional Top Table

as I would like to reassure you that everyone will make an effort for your big day, unfortunately that can't be guaranteed!

If your two sets of parents have never met before, you might like to switch the dads around so that your parents are seated together. If parents are divorced, it's polite to include any new spouses on the top table, usually sitting next to their partner. If you think there may be ruffled hierarchy feathers, choose a round top table – who is sitting where is less obvious and chatting will be much easier.

If you have a complicated family situation or several members of the main bridal party just don't get along, you can forget the top table altogether and seat parents with their own family and friends. You can then choose a top table for just the two of you.

Other tips for a successful seating plan include:

- seating your officiant with members of the bridal party, usually with one set of parents
- putting family together (as long as they get along)
- making a boy-girl-boy-girl arrangement – it often works well and keeps conversation flowing
- seating work colleagues together
- putting people with similar interests and of similar ages together
- to keep conversations fresh, asking each male guest to swap places with the male guest to his right after the main course
- putting a single guest who knows nobody on a table with a chatty friend of a similar age or profession and asking him or her to make sure the other guest feels welcome

The seating plan

Use this handy sheet to help you work out who to sit where at the reception.

Top table

1. ______
2. ______
3. ______
4. ______
5. ______
6. ______

7. ______
8. ______
9. ______
10. ______
11. ______
12. ______

Table two

1. ______
2. ______
3. ______
4. ______
5. ______
6. ______

7. ______
8. ______
9. ______
10. ______
11. ______
12. ______

Table three

1. ______
2. ______
3. ______
4. ______
5. ______
6. ______

7. ______
8. ______
9. ______
10. ______
11. ______
12. ______

Photocopy this sheet as many times as you need

Table four

1.	7.
2.	8.
3.	9.
4.	10.
5.	11.
6.	12.

Table five

1.	7.
2.	8.
3.	9.
4.	10.
5.	11.
6.	12.

Table six

1.	7.
2.	8.
3.	9.
4.	10.
5.	11.
6.	12.

Table seven

1.	7.
2.	8.
3.	9.
4.	10.
5.	11.
6.	12.

Photocopy this sheet as many times as you need

Table eight

1.	7.
2.	8.
3.	9.
4.	10.
5.	11.
6.	12.

Table nine

1.	7.
2.	8.
3.	9.
4.	10.
5.	11.
6.	12.

Table ten

1.	7.
2.	8.
3.	9.
4.	10.
5.	11.
6.	12.

Table eleven

1.	7.
2.	8.
3.	9.
4.	10.
5.	11.
6.	12.

Photocopy this sheet as many times as you need

Table twelve

1.	7.
2.	8.
3.	9.
4.	10.
5.	11.
6.	12.

Table thirteen

1.	7.
2.	8.
3.	9.
4.	10.
5.	11.
6.	12.

Table fourteen

1.	7.
2.	8.
3.	9.
4.	10.
5.	11.
6.	12.

Table fifteen

1.	7.
2.	8.
3.	9.
4.	10.
5.	11.
6.	12.

Photocopy this sheet as many times as you need

Tables and favours

The traditional table will be set for anything up to 12 guests, with some sort of centrepiece decoration of either fruit or flowers. Keep the centrepieces low so guests can talk over them or high enough that your guests can chat underneath. Each table will usually have one or more printed menus with a list of the food and wines you'll be serving.

Whether or not to put a favour at each place setting is up to you and your budget. The traditional five sugared almonds representing health, wealth, fertility, happiness and longevity are often replaced these days with anything from lottery tickets to mini bottles of whisky emblazoned with the wedding date and the happy couple's initials. A token gift to say welcome and thanks for coming is a nice touch but is definitely not expected, so don't feel obliged if it's something you really can't afford.

You'll need to either name or number each table and, unless the wedding is very small, have a table plan close to the entrance listing the guests seated at each table. Name cards for each guest are a must so they can easily find their seat.

Your reception timetable

This will give you some idea of what happens and when at the traditional dinner and dancing type of reception. It's up to you which parts to include and which to leave out.

4.00pm Arrive at the reception

The wedding party arrives at the reception followed by the guests.

4.00–4.30pm The receiving line

The bride, groom and main wedding party form a receiving line and greet guests one by one. Many couples choose not to have a receiving line, feeling it's too formal and time-consuming. Guests should be welcomed with a glass of bubbly or a cocktail.

4.30–5.30pm Cocktails

The bride and groom go off with members of the main bridal party for photographs. Guests enjoy a drink and canapés and check the table plan for where they will be sitting. Background music is often played.

5.45pm Announcements

The toastmaster or head waiter announces dinner and guests take their seats. Both sets of parents, the best man and the bridesmaids usually go in first, followed by the other guests. The bride and groom are announced and guests stand as they enter.

The first dance

All eyes will be on you as you take to the floor so it's worth having a dance lesson or at least practising a few steps beforehand.

Here are a few classics that are always popular:

Beauty and the Beast .... *Celine Dion and Peabo Bryson*
Can You Feel the Love Tonight? .... *Elton John*
Endless Love .... *Diana Ross and Lionel Richie*
The First Time Ever I Saw Your Face .. *Roberta Flack*
Fly Me to the Moon .... *Frank Sinatra*
Forever .... *Nat King Cole*
The Greatest Love of All .... *Whitney Houston*
A Groovy Kind of Love .... *Phil Collins*
How Sweet It Is .... *James Taylor*
I Do .... *Natalie Cole*
It Had to Be You .... *Harry Connick Jr*
My Girl .... *The Temptations*
Only You .... *The Platters*
Truly, Madly, Deeply.......................... *Savage Garden*

6.00pm Welcome

When the bride and groom are seated and the room is quiet, the father of the bride or the toastmaster welcomes everyone to the wedding. A minister may say a blessing.

6.15pm Dinner is served

The first course is served to the top table, then to all the other guests. Other courses follow in good but not rushed time.

7.45pm Toasts

After dessert, glasses are refilled and the bride's father toasts the health of the bride and groom.

7.50pm The speeches

The father of the bride makes the first speech and is followed by the groom, who responds on behalf of himself and his new wife. The groom proposes a toast to the bridesmaids and may also give out small thank-you presents to the bridesmaids, flower girls and any page boys and to his and the bride's mothers and anyone else who has made a major contribution to the wedding planning. The best man replies on behalf of the bridesmaids and then makes his speech. If the bride wants to say a few words – a growing trend – she can do this at the same time or just after her husband.

8.30pm Cutting the cake

The bride and groom cut the cake, which is then served with coffee. Any evening-only guests will usually be invited to arrive just after the cake has been cut and should be welcomed with a drink.

8.45pm The first dance

Tables are cleared to make way for dancing. The bride and groom take to the floor for their chosen first dance tune. The next dance is for the bride and her father and the groom and his mother. Other guests gradually take to the floor after the first couple of minutes.

10.00pm+ Departure of the bride and groom

Depending on your preference and the venue, the evening will draw to a close at a set time or may go on until dawn. If you do anticipate partying into the night, remember to make it clear to your guests that you won't be leaving – there is a tradition that the guests stay until after the bride and groom leave, and older friends and those with small children will want to go home.

At an agreed time before too many guests have left, it's fun to indulge in that age-old tradition of tossing the bouquet. All the single girls crowd around the bride, who turns away from them and tosses her bouquet backwards. According to tradition, whoever catches it will be the next to marry.

The speeches

The key questions

Q Who makes a speech? **The traditional wedding includes a selection of speeches to thank major role players as well as entertain the guests. They take place once the food is over and before the cake cutting ceremony and coffee is served. The usual running order is the bride's father followed by the groom (and perhaps the bride), then the best man.**

Q Should the bride give a speech? **Some modern brides say a few words at the same time as their groom. It's up to you what form this takes. You can either join your groom in thanking your guests for coming, your parents for their involvement and for the help of major players such as your bridesmaids. Or you could be a little more adventurous and make it very personal by saying a few heartfelt words including a surprise for your groom. You could even go as far as actress Catherine Zeta-Jones by singing a song dedicated to the man you love!**

Q Must there be speeches? **There's nothing to say you have to have any formal speeches as part of your reception – even though the best man's speech is a considered a highlight for many guests. If you are having a very informal event, agree beforehand that just your groom will speak. He will still want to formally thank bridesmaids and parents – and perhaps give each of them a gift – but at the same time announce that you wanted the day to be as informal as possible so you'll be giving traditional speeches a miss.**

Q How are toasts different to speeches? **After the formal speeches from the father of the bride, the groom and best man, increasingly other guests want to offer their own toasts to the bride and groom. These are usually short, just a heart-felt line or two or even a joke about marriage. They tend to come after the best man has finished and are the perfect chance for the father of the groom and the chief bridesmaid to have their say.**

Not everyone is happy to speak in public and you need to reassure anyone expected to make a dreaded wedding speech that an Oscar-winning performance, whilst fabulous, is not expected! Sincerity, with the odd funny anecdote if they can manage it, will suffice.

Speakers need to speak slowly and clearly, projecting their voices so that the guests at the back of the room can hear. Get your groom, dad or best man to practise a couple of times beforehand. Asking an impartial friend to give an honest appraisal if they are mumbling or racing their words is always a good idea as well.

The father of the bride

- Thanks guests for coming.
- Says a few heartwarming words about his wonderful daughter and how pleased he is to be welcoming the groom into the family.
- Proposes a toast to the couple and their future happiness.

The groom

- Thanks the father of the bride for his speech and the toast.
- Says something about how happy he is to be married to his beautiful new wife.
- Gives out thank-you gifts to the best man, ushers, bridesmaids, both mothers and anyone else who has helped out.
- Proposes a toast to the bridesmaids.

The bride

- You may like to think about making a bride's speech – and why not? – in which case you should speak with, or just after the groom.
- Some brides write or recite a love poem, sing a song or just tell a little story about their groom – whatever will make your guests smile.

The best man

- Thanks the groom on behalf of the bridesmaids and other attendants for his kind words.
- Launches into 5–7 minutes of banter that largely revolves around anecdotes about the groom in his past life. May involve props or even a short film.
- Proposes a toast to the bride and groom.

Suggest that anyone making a speech puts key phrases on to cue cards and to number each card so they remain in the correct order. Cards usually work better than writing out every word, which would mean looking down the whole time and being tempted to speak too quickly.

Template speech: the father of the bride

For the dad who hasn't a clue where to start, a few handy words to get him going.

Good afternoon ladies and gentlemen.
I'm delighted to welcome you all here today to celebrate the marriage between my beautiful daughter **[name of bride]** and **[name of groom]**.

Thank you all so much for joining our families on this wonderful occasion. **[Insert thoughts on the ceremony, what it has meant to the family.]**

I have to take a moment and say how beautiful my daughter looks today. I have never seen her looking so radiant. **[Name of groom]**, you are a lucky man. You had better look after her or you'll be answering to me!

[Insert funny/touching story about the groom asking permission to marry daughter or feelings when they announced their engagement.]

I would also like to offer you both a few words of wisdom on the subject of enjoying a happy marriage. For a start, she's always right and you're always wrong! **[Funny/touching anecdote on the secrets of a successful marriage, children, money and so on.]**

Just before I sit down I would also like to thank our fabulous venue today. I hope you all enjoyed the wonderful meal. Congratulations to **[name of caterer/venue]**. Your team has done an amazing job and everything was delicious.

Now all that remains is for me to ask you all to be upstanding to toast the future health and happiness of **[names of bride and groom]**. The bride and groom.

[Introduce the groom to give his speech.]

Template speech: the groom

For the nervous groom, use this handy template to start him off.

Good afternoon ladies and gentleman.

I've been told that this is one of the only times in a man's life when he can be in the company of his wife and mother-in-law and not be interrupted **[pause]** I may be here some time! **[Or similar amusing words or an anecdote to set a light-hearted tone.]**

I'd like to take this opportunity to thank **[name of father-in-law]** for his kind words. I am delighted to be joining the **[name of wife's family]** family and rest assured I will treasure **[name of wife]** for ever.

[Funny story about asking father-in-law's permission to marry his daughter, if appropriate.]

May I join **[name of father-in-law]** in thanking everyone for being here today with my wife and me. We feel privileged to have had so many good friends with us as we took the momentous step of becoming husband and wife. **[Make an observation about the ceremony, the day so far, what it has meant to you.]**

Before I say thank you to our wonderful bridesmaids I would just like to say a few words about my beautiful new wife. **[Insert heartfelt, funny story about meeting your wife, the proposal, her wedding obsessions and so on.]**

Now on behalf of **[name of wife]** and I we would like to thank those very special people who have helped to make our day complete. Any wedding involves a lot of hard work and we are eternally grateful for their help.

First I would like to propose a toast to the bridesmaids. The bridesmaids **[toast, then add something about how lovely they look, how much they have helped his wife]. [Each bridesmaid can be asked up in turn to receive a small gift.]**

I would also like to say a huge thank you and propose a toast to our parents. Your love and support means the world to us. **[Toast the bride's parents, naming them, then the groom's parents.]**

[This may also be an appropriate time to mention 'absent friends', including a deceased friend or relative.]

Finally, I would like to say thank you to my best man – although I may be reconsidering this once he has given his speech! **[Name of best man]**, you have been my rock for many years and we have shared many adventures, but more of that to come, no doubt! So cheers, **[name of best man]**, for your support throughout today.

[Introduce the best man to give his speech.]

Your notes

Template speech: the best man

Words of wisdom to set him on the right track.

Ladies and gentlemen, I would like to thank **[name of groom]** on behalf of the bridesmaids for his **[kind/brief/heartfelt]** words. I agree that they all look **[lovely/sweet/drunk]**. I was **[honoured/shocked/confused]** when **[name of groom]** asked me to be his best man and presumed everyone else had said no. Even **[name of least likely guest]** said he had joined the **[Foreign Legion/a monastery]** and couldn't possibly oblige. So here I am, and where do I start?

I first met **[name of groom]** when we were both **[at school/in the pub/at reform school]** when his nickname was **[if none, make one up]** and we immediately became **[great friends/drinking buddies/rivals]**. Since that time things have got progressively **[better/worse]**. We have been through many things together, including **[puberty/drinking/partying]** and most memorable of all was when we were **[age]** and **[name of groom]** got into **[amusing anecdote]**. Things didn't get much better either, when **[number]** years later he also **[amusing anecdote]**.

And at last we come to the stag night. From what I can recall, it all started off sedately but ended up in drunken debauchery **[story from stag night]** when **[name of groom]** ended up **[naked/in jail/tied to a lamppost]**.

It was **[years]** ago when **[name of groom]** met **[name of bride]**, the **[best/worst]** thing that ever happened to him. It was **[love/lust]** at first sight. It took **[name of groom]** **[number of days/weeks/months/years]** to pluck up the courage to ask **[name of bride]** to go **[on a date/to bed]** and the rest is history.

I ask you now to raise your glasses and join me in a final toast to our wonderful bride and groom. To Mr and Mrs **[name]**. May their life together bring them much happiness.

Ideas for entertainment

It's expected at a traditional wedding reception that you'll provide your guests with some kind of entertainment. This can take the form of a live band, a disco, a string quartet and/or recorded music as well as entertainers such as magicians. As with everything else, it's up to your taste and your budget.

A five-piece band is perfect for a smart evening reception in a hotel, whereas a good DJ with a deck is suitable for more informal surroundings such as a marquee. A close-up magician moving from table to table as your guests are eating is always popular. Face painters and even clowns will go down well with younger guests. If you hire any kind of entertainment, make sure you have seen and heard them perform before you book. If they will be providing music, it's a good idea to ask for a play list or provide one of your own, bearing in mind that you need to appeal to all musical tastes and the wide age range of your guests.

Five tips to keep your guests smiling

1 Set up a wedding website so guests can find venue details, directions, places to stay and gift list information. After the wedding you can post pictures on to the site.
2 Make sure your guests have something to eat and drink while you have your photographs taken. It can take over an hour and they will be thirsty.
3 Keep everyone in the know about timings – when food will be served, what time the dancing should start, what time the party is due to finish.
4 As far as possible, seat people with people they know. It's good to mingle but pretty boring to be stuck on a table of strangers.
5 Plan the dance music carefully, with a good smattering of old favourites that are guaranteed to fill the floor. Have a quiet room where people can go to chat if they want to.

Dressed to Thrill

Choosing your wedding dress is one of life's truly magical moments, and finding the perfect outfits for the rest of the bridal party is almost as important for a great looking day. So get ready and let's go shopping!

The key questions

Q What will suit the formality of the wedding? **You need to bear in mind the style of wedding when you choose your dress. A church wedding needs covered shoulders (even if it's a jacket you take off later). A Cinderella-style ball gown will look a little out of place in a contemporary setting such as a register office or city hotel.**

Q What is your personal style? **You need to feel like a princess in your wedding dress and you should love your outfit. Work with the dress designer or look at off-the-peg gowns that suit your style; big dresses aren't for everyone and your figure may not be up to slim and slinky. A short dress or trouser suit may even end up being your favourite look.**

Q What will your groom want to wear? **Find out early on what your man wants to wear. His choices are simpler: a formal wedding means a (usually hired) tailcoat, waistcoat and trousers; a civil or contemporary ceremony means a suit. Just remember, the groom's outfit dictates what the rest of the men at the wedding will wear too.**

Q How do you want your attendants to look? **Again it's all down to the formality of the wedding and how many attendants you are having. The good news is that bridesmaids no longer have to wear exactly**

the same dresses. Co-ordinating rather than matching outfits is the key. And don't forget the mums in all the excitement; it's a big day for them too and they'll want to look their best.

Q What can your budget afford? **It's easy to get carried away and blow a big proportion of the wedding budget on that dream dress. The good news is that the high street is packed with affordable wedding outfits – for the whole bridal party – and you can look great without busting your budget.**

The wedding dress

Before you start shopping, have a good look through some wedding magazines such as *You & Your Wedding* and *Cosmopolitan Bride* to get an idea of the sort of dresses you like. Think about how much you want to spend and what sort of accessories you'll also need to buy. Don't forget all the elements of your outfit.

- Wedding dress
- Headdress
- Veil
- Shoes
- Lingerie
- Hosiery
- Earrings
- Necklace
- Wrap/bolero
- Handbag
- Garter

You can buy a wedding dress from many different places and can pay anything from a few hundreds to many thousands of pounds. Think about what you want to get out of each visit and go armed with a few questions to get the most out of every shopping trip.

Things to think about when you are shopping for your wedding dress

- Does the shop feel welcoming and are the assistants friendly and helpful?
- Does it stock dresses in a range of prices with plenty of choice for your budget?
- Does it custom-make dresses and/or have a good range of off-the-peg dresses in styles you like?
- Can it order a sample of a dress that you have seen in a magazine?
- Does it sell accessories?
- Does it sell bridesmaids' dresses?
- How long will it take to have a dress made after placing an order?
- Do you have to pay extra for alterations?
- Do you have to pay a deposit? When is the balance due? Do they offer a payment plan?
- What is the cancellation policy?

Bridal shops

All the big-name bridal designers and manufacturers sell their custom-made dresses though one or more of these shops. They usually stock a range of bridesmaids' outfits as well as shoes and accessories so you can buy everything under one roof.

You'll usually have to make an appointment to try on a wedding dress, but don't let this put you off. It's actually for your benefit so you get space in a fitting room and the attention of one of the staff who'll be able to advise you on what is available and on things such as fittings and alterations.

This is the most expensive wedding dress option because they use the best fabrics and trained sales assistants. The dress will also be made to fit you, which is why you can't just go in and buy 'off the peg' and will need to allow anything up to nine months to have the dress made.

Once you've chosen your dream dress, expect to leave a deposit and schedule a series of fitting appointments. Make sure you find out exactly what is included in the quoted price, and work out a final date when your dress will be ready for collection.

Shopping in the high street

With most of the major department stores now stocking bridal wear, you can buy a gorgeous dress for a very reasonable price. The important thing is not the price tag but that you feel fabulous.

If you are a standard size you can probably go in, try on a range of styles and buy a dress on the same day. If the dress needs minor alteration, such as taking up, most shops will be able to arrange this for you for a small extra charge or recommend a local seamstress that they work with. It's best not to choose a dress that needs major alteration, even if you know a good dressmaker. Cheaper dresses are mass-produced, usually in the Far East, and the fabric and seams are not made to be altered in the same way as a designer dress, so be careful as the dress could easily be ruined.

Most bridal wear departments also stock a good range of bridesmaids' dresses for all ages and affordable accessories like bags, headdresses and shoes.

Dressmakers

If you have a vision of your perfect dress but the designer prices are just too much, you could get a dressmaker to make it for you. You buy the fabric and between you come up with a design – probably using pictures from magazines with a little bit of one dress mixed with a little bit of another. This is not the cheapest option but it will save you a lot on the designer prices.

Buying online

The number of wedding dresses to buy on the web has soared with the increase in online shopping. Sites such as eBay are brimming with everything from gowns and shoes to tiaras and veils, all at seemingly great prices. But it's a risky process; many of the dresses will be shipped from the Far East, so you need to be sure of what you're ordering and whether it's likely to fit before parting with your money. And most website sellers don't offer refunds, so there's no chance of getting your money back.

Dress shopping tips

- Try to avoid shopping on busy Saturdays when you may not get the best service.
- Take along someone whose opinion you trust. Limit the shopping party to four people including you.
- Feel free to shop on your own for the first couple of appointments, inviting mothers and bridesmaids once you have a shortlist.
- Wear supportive lingerie and take along a strapless bra and a pair of shoes with roughly the heel height you are thinking of wearing.
- Keep your budget firmly in mind. Trying on dresses way out of your price bracket will just be depressing.
- Try on a variety of styles; many have little hanger-appeal but look great once they are on.
- Take advice from the sales persons – they should know what they're talking about – but don't be bullied.
- If one dress is not quite right, ask if the same designer has a similar style perhaps with a different neckline or sleeves that you may like better. Shops won't stock every style but they may be able to get in something different for you.
- Even if you spend a long time in one shop, don't feel you have to buy anything.
- Don't buy on your first shopping trip. It's best to take time to reflect – you can always go back if you were lucky enough to have found 'the one' first time out!

Appointment card
Date
Time
Fitting 1
Fitting 2

Dressed to Thrill

Your Wedding Gifts

Your Honeymoon

One Week and Counting

End-of-season sales

All the main bridal designers hold regular sample sales, usually at the end of each season, when they sell off old stock and shop samples at greatly reduced prices. Keep an eye on individual websites and ask favourite shops for dates of expected sales. If you are a standard size 8–12 you can pick up an amazing bargain. The dresses are likely to be a bit dirty but you'll have made enough of a saving to pay for specialist cleaning.

Going for vintage

Wearing your mother's wedding dress is guaranteed to add a very personal touch to your day. Providing you are much the same size and the style of the dress can be subtly altered and updated, this is a lovely idea. Alternatively, keep an eye out at second-hand and charity shops for vintage dresses. As long as the fabric is still in good condition and you are adept with a needle or have a clever seamstress friend you could have a unique dress at a fabulous price.

The informal approach

As informal, contemporary weddings become more popular, an increasing number of brides are simply choosing a stunning dress they love. You can buy an appropriate mid-length or evening dress from one of the mainstream designer's latest collections for the same price, or cheaper, than many wedding dresses. The summer collections in particular will feature lots of choice in white, ivory and pastels.

The shapes and silhouettes

You'll want a style that makes you look your best, so think about the most flattering styles for your figure before you start shopping.

Dress shapes

A-line: The most flattering style so it's no surprise that this is the most popular shape of wedding gown. The dress will gently flare out from the shoulders and suits most figure shapes, whether you are short or tall.

Ball gown: The ultimate fairytale dress with a narrow fitted waistline and a full, flowing skirt. It's a 'big' dress so tends to suit taller girls.
Empire: Cut a bit like a maternity dress with a high waistline that starts just below the bust. The skirt is usually slim and flowing. Avoid this style if you have a very full bust as it can make you look pregnant.
Princess: Another popular shape that suits most figure types. Vertical panels of fabric follow the natural contours of the body to give a flattering outline.
Sheath: Simple and elegant, this style of dress follows the natural curves of the body from shoulder to hem. They are usually in fairly clingy, figure-hugging fabrics so don't really suit either very slender or very curvy forms.

Skirt styles

Bouffant: A very wide skirt, often on a hoop to make it even bigger. A clever way to disguise big hips, provided you have a neat waist.
Box pleats: Deep parallel pleats of fabric that cascade down the skirt. Flattering for most figures and they work well with heavier fabrics such as duchesse silk or satin.
Bustle: The fabric is gathered below the waistline at the back of the dress to create fullness. Flattering to most figure types and it doesn't make your bottom look bigger!
Pick-up hem: An elegant look where pieces of fabric gather and drape in a curve at several points around the hem to give a slightly scooped effect.
Trumpet: Sophisticated and flirty at the same time, the skirt is slim and hugging until it reaches mid-thigh, where it flares out to finish just below the knee.

Necklines

Boat: Sits just below the collar bone and goes straight across the chest. It can be used with or without sleeves and works well if you want to minimize a large bust.
Contessa: An off-the-shoulder neckline that attaches to the sleeves to form a continuous line across the arms and chest. It flatters long, slender necks and well-defined shoulders.

Halterneck: Formed with two pieces of fabric that go up from the waist or bust and join at the back of the neck. A sleek, sexy and informal look that works well if you don't have to wear a bra.
Illusion high: The neckline is made of sheer fabric such as lace or chiffon, which fits snugly against the neck and usually covers the arms as well. A formal look that is sexy without being over the top.
Portrait: A shawl-like collar that wraps around the shoulders. It is a popular style because of how well it frames the face.
Scoop: A softly rounded neckline that slopes across the collar bones. Pretty and demure as long as the scoop isn't cut too deep.
Sleeveless: The back and front attach at the shoulder with narrow pieces of fabric. A young and sophisticated look but you need toned upper arms.
Square: Similar to the scoop neckline but more elegant and formal.
Strapless: A hugely popular style where arms and shoulders are bare and you rely on gravity and a good bra to keep you covered.
Sweetheart: Another popular shape where the neckline dips down to a point into the cleavage. A romantic style that suits most figure types.

What will suit your shape?

Fuller figure: Choose a long, A-line or simple shape and avoid anything too clingy. Long or sheer sleeves will flatter your arms and a V-neckline will make less of a full bust.
Small bust: Look for dresses with decoration such as bows or flowers around the neckline.
Petite: You want to elongate your body so look for a sheath or princess-line dress. Be wary of full skirts, which may overwhelm your shape.
Hourglass: You want a dress that emphasises your waist and flatters your bust and hips. A V-neckline or off-the-shoulder dress will lessen a full bust and a corset top with fuller skirt will slim the hips.
Large tummy/thighs: The empire line hides all sorts of figure flaws, flowing from the bust and giving a leaner silhouette.

Bridal accessories

Once you have found your perfect dress you'll want to think about accessories. Your headdress, veil, shoes and lingerie are all important parts of putting together a total look.

Headdresses

Most brides will want to wear something in their hair and if you wear a veil you'll need some sort of accessory to secure it. There are lots of options from the plain to full-on glamour. Make sure whatever you choose is comfortable and secure – you don't want to be worried that it might fall off.

Alice band: Plain or decorated with a bow or pearls, this is a simple easy-to-wear accessory that looks pretty and modern without being overly fussy.

Clips and combs: Ideal if you want a little decoration but nothing too fancy, they can be used to secure an up-do or a veil. They are sometimes decorated with diamanté or pearls.

Crown: A must for any fairytale bride but they can be tricky to keep on and you might need professional help to pin it securely.

Hat: For an informal wedding, particularly in a register office, a hat is a stylish option and will be perfect if you are wearing a simple dress and hate the thought of a veil.

Tiara: This is the classic bridal headdress and works with any style of dress and just about any hairstyle, up or down. Choose from simple bands to ornate creations. Do make sure the tiara fits your head snugly so it doesn't keep slipping forwards.

Veils

The veil comes in and out of fashion but for a traditional bride it is a must-have on her wedding day. Buy your veil once you have found your dress, perhaps reflecting a detail from the day such as a lace edge or pearl trim. If you want something special, your dress designer should be able to make a veil that perfectly matches the style of your dress. Alternatively, most bridal shops and department stores have a good selection to choose from.

Ballet: A floor length veil made of several simple layers, often worn very long to double up as a train.

Blusher: A short, usually single layer veil that reaches to the shoulders. It often comes attached to a hair comb.

Fingertip: Probably the most popular choice, with several layers of fabric extending to the fingertips.

Mantilla: A traditional Spanish-inspired lace veil worn without a headdress and simply draped over the head to frame the face.

Waterfall: A very romantic look with several layers of veiling attached to a hairband that cascades down to the hip or knees. The top layer is often short so can easily be turned back once you reach the altar.

Gloves

A pretty pair of gloves in silk, satin, lace or even the softest leather can look great with certain styles of wedding dress. Take the glove off your left hand when exchanging rings or you can give them both to your chief bridesmaid to hold until after the register is signed.

Gloves are usually worn only during the ceremony and for the photographs. Take them off at the reception and when you greet and shake hands with your guests.

Shoes

A great pair of wedding shoes will have you walking on air but they have to be comfortable too – you could be standing for anything up to 10 hours! If you aren't used to wearing high heels, your wedding day isn't the time to start. A 5 cm/2 in heel is the most comfortable height and will work with most styles of dress.

Choose your shoes before any final dress fittings to ensure

the heel height works with the length of the dress. Many bridal shops will keep a range of shoes with varying heels for you wear when trying on a dress but for final fittings you should have your own shoes with you.

Jewellery

Every bride will want to wear some jewellery but err on the side of less is more – you don't want to look theatrical. If your dress is heavily decorated, a simple pendant or string of pearls will suffice. A simple dress can be worn with a bigger necklace like a choker or perhaps drop-earrings or gloves.

Bridal lingerie

Well-fitting lingerie can make all the difference to how your dress looks so it's important you choose something that's comfortable but also works with the style of your gown.

Bra: Most wedding dresses will look better worn with a bra. Even if your dress has skinny straps, a low back or is strapless there are plenty of suitable bras that will give you invisible support. If your dress is very low-cut and you are small-busted you can probably get away with using bra tape – flesh-coloured tape that you stick on to your skin for a little extra support.
Bustier: A long-line alternative to a bra, often sold in the bridal shops, which comes down to the top of your knickers and can be used with stockings. They are usually heavily boned and offer good support for the fuller figure.
Bodyshaper: A little bit of Lycra is a great idea if you want to create a smooth silhouette and look a couple of pounds lighter. Wear it a couple of times before the wedding just to be sure you are comfortable.
Knickers and thongs: Whatever style of pants you wear, functionality is much more important than whether they look sexy. Plain knickers are less likely to show than anything decorated, and flesh-coloured underwear is a better choice than white.
Hosiery: Tights, stockings or hold-ups, the choice is yours but again comfort is the most important factor. The most flattering wedding hosiery is a natural or nude shade rather than white. And don't forget the garter!

The bride's outfit

Keep track of your wedding outfit and those all-important accessories.

Shop/designer

- Contact name
- E-mail
- Telephone number
- Website
- Date for fitting 1
- Date for fitting 2
- Date for fitting 3
- Dress delivery date

Item	Deposit	Total cost
Wedding dress		£
Alteration cost		£
Headdress		£
Veil		£
Shoes		£
Gloves		£
Wrap/bolero		£
Lingerie		£
Hosiery		£
Necklace		£
Earrings		£
Garter		£
Other		£

Dressed to Thrill | Your Wedding Gifts | Your Honeymoon | One Week and Counting

Wedding rings

Your wedding band will probably become your most important piece of jewellery since it symbolises the moment you became man and wife. You may have chosen this ring at the same time as your engagement ring or may be buying it just before the wedding.

When you choose your wedding ring always wear your engagement ring so you know they'll fit neatly together and feel comfortable. If you have a gold engagement ring you are most likely to choose a hard-wearing 18ct gold band; if your engagement ring is platinum you'll need to buy a platinum band so they complement one another. Weddings bands are traditionally quite plain but many modern styles incorporate diamonds – lovely if your budget allows!

Your groom may or may not want to wear a ring but, either way, allow enough time before the wedding to get your ring or rings engraved with your initials, the wedding date or a simple love note to one another.

Something old, something new

Something old: To take from your past life. A piece of family jewellery or an inherited Bible are often used.

Something new: To celebrate your new married life. Just about everything you'll be wearing will be new so this one is easy!

Something borrowed: This is usually taken from a happily married friend in the hope that some of their good fortune will rub off on you. A handkerchief, earrings or a bracelet are popular choices.

Something blue: Blue is the colour of fidelity. Think about having bluebells in your bouquet, a blue bow on your garter or sapphire earrings (which could be borrowed and do both jobs!).

Looking the part

The key questions

Q Can you dictate how your guests dress at your wedding? Much as you may like to tell everyone to wear a particular style or colour, it would be unreasonable to expect your guests to follow a strict dress code. The formality of the wedding will be dictated by the style of your invitation and the type of reception you have planned. A church wedding is the most formal wedding and men will usually wear dark suits and most of the women will think about wearing a hat (although hats are no longer compulsory). The men in the main bridal party will take their lead from the groom; if he is wearing formal wear then the fathers of the bride and groom, the best man and the ushers are all expected to follow suit

Q Is black tie a good idea? If you are having a late afternoon ceremony and want a grand evening reception, then specifying black tie on the invitation is a stylish idea. Male guests will then be expected to wear a tuxedo and bow tie and the women will wear cocktail or full-length evening dresses. Do bear in mind that this type of event will often involve your male guests hiring their suits, which is expensive, and be prepared for a few guests not to follow your dress code.

Q Should female guests wear black at a wedding? It used to be considered unsuitable for wedding guests to wear black dresses but these days attitudes are more relaxed and it is perfectly acceptable. In fact, many adult bridesmaids wear black dresses with the addition of colourful accessories for evening and winter weddings. When it comes to wearing white, most guests will hopefully not want to be mistaken for the bride and will steer well clear of any outfit that looks remotely like bridal attire.

Dressing the bridal party

Style of wedding	Bridesmaids	Groom/best man	Mothers
Formal (sit-down meal)	Long dress, jewellery, posy	Formal wear or black tie	Glamorous suit or long dress, elaborate headpiece
Semi-formal (sit-down or buffet)	Long or short dress, posy	Formal wear or a day suit	Elegant suit and hat
Contemporary (buffet or cocktail party)	Short cocktail dress, posy or handbag	Suit or blazer and trousers	Stylish short dress, optional hat

Your bridesmaids' outfits

Frilly satin nightmares are a thing of the past – fashion has finally caught up with the bridesmaid dress and you'll have a vast choice of gorgeous party styles to choose from! You may be able to buy your maids' dresses from the same place as your wedding dress. Otherwise check out department stores for reasonably priced ideas – and do try the evening wear section, which may have just what you're looking for.

Your bridesmaids are bound to be different ages, shapes and sizes and it's often a good idea to let them wear similar but not identical dresses. If the colour and the length are the same you'll be able to achieve a well co-ordinated look. It is much more important that your maids feel comfortable with their outfits – it's always going to be very difficult to find one style of dress that suits everyone.

Bridesmaids' accessories tend to be simple, perhaps an Alice band or a floral hair comb, and they will most likely carry a simple posy of fresh flowers. It looks good if all your maids wear the same style of shoes, which can be dyed to match the dresses by many of the specialist shoe companies.

Try to choose your bridesmaids' dresses about six months before the wedding, after you've finalised your own dress. It's traditional for your maids to pay for their own outfits so do bear this in mind when shopping. It's fine for you to have your say, but if you fall in love with a particularly expensive style you may need to offer to contribute towards the cost.

Many brides give their maids their outfits as a gift, which doubles as a thank-you present for participating in the big day.

Junior attendants

Little bridesmaids, flower girls and page boys need to look cute but feel comfortable in what they are wearing, otherwise you're in for trouble! The bride usually makes suggestions about the general style and colour she would like smaller attendants to wear but, since their parents are footing the bill, you'll need to get their input too before making any final decisions. Don't forget that little ones grow quickly, so don't be in too much of a hurry to buy their wedding outfit. There's no way it'll still fit in 12 months.

Little girls

Young bridesmaids and flower girls should reflect the colour scheme and general look of the older maids. White dresses are the most popular choice, with a coloured sash and trimmings in the wedding theme. Other options are velvet for a winter wedding or a pinafore dress for a summer wedding. Bridesmaids' dresses can be pricey, particularly when bought from a bridal boutique, so don't forget to look in the local children's wear shops and at department store collections so you are aware of everything on offer.

Little boys

Traditional outfits for page boys and ring bearers were velvet suits with short trousers, jacket and a white shirt. These days most young boys will feel happier in a scaled-down version of what the rest of the men in the bridal party are wearing. Many formal wear shops offer suits from tiny to teenagers and there is something very cute about youngsters in this style of dress.

Mothers of the bride and groom

It's a big day for both mothers and they'll want to dress to impress. There is a lot of choice and to a certain extent what they wear will be dictated by the formality of the wedding. Evening dress is suitable for a late afternoon ceremony and formal reception. A shift dress with a matching coat, a coatdress or a longer dress teamed with a little jacket are all popular styles for afternoon and evening celebrations. If they feel more comfortable in something more contemporary, a softly tailored trouser suit in a pastel shade is great for all but the most formal of weddings.

Most mothers will also want to wear some sort of hat or at least one of the latest colourful headdresses adorned with feathers in a complementary colour to her outfit.

The mother of the bride usually tells the groom's mother the colour and general style of her outfit before the wedding. This is not to say that they have to follow the same style of dress; the most important thing is that they both feel comfortable and confident in what they are wearing. If either of them is feeling a little daunted about being the centre of attention, think about treating them to a confidence-boosting spa day where they can pick up lots of hair and make-up tips in a relaxed setting.

Attendants' outfits

To track what each of the bride's attendants will be wearing and what it will all cost (if you're paying!).

	Make/colour/style	Cost
Chief bridesmaid		£
Dress		£
Shoes		£
Headdress		£
Wrap/bolero		£
Jewellery		£
Flowers		£
Bridesmaid 1		£
Dress		£
Shoes		£
Headdress		£
Wrap/bolero		£
Jewellery		£
Flowers		£
Bridesmaid 2		£
Dress		£
Shoes		£
Headdress		£
Wrap/bolero		£
Jewellery		£
Flowers		£

	Make/colour/style	Cost
Bridesmaid 3		£
Dress		£
Shoes		£
Headdress		£
Wrap/bolero		£
Jewellery		£
Flowers		£
Flower girl 1		£
Dress		£
Shoes		£
Jewellery		£
Flowers		£
Flower girl 2		£
Dress		£
Shoes		£
Jewellery		£
Flowers		£
Page boy/ring bearer		£
Suit		£
Shoes		£
Accessories		£

Your notes

Dressed to Thrill

Your Wedding Gifts

Your Honeymoon

One Week and Counting

The groom's outfit

The key questions

Q How formal is the wedding? The traditional groom's outfit is either formal wear (morning coat, trousers, shirt and cravat) or a smart dark-coloured lounge suit. Formal wear, which can be bought or hired, is the usual choice for a church wedding and an ordinary suit more appropriate for a civil ceremony.

Q Do you want all the men dressed the same? The male members of the main bridal party (best man, fathers of the bride and groom and the ushers) should wear the same style of outfit as the groom, with accessories such as a waistcoat following the same colour scheme. If the groom is wearing an ordinary suit, then the men can wear suits of their own choice, though they should preferably be black or navy.

Q What are the most modern suit options? A wedding is the chance for your groom to splash out on a fabulous designer suit – the outfit he normally wears for the office just isn't good enough, even for an informal wedding! Colour choices should be black or navy and a single-breasted suit is currently the most fashionable option. Several of the leading suit designers have diffusion ranges at high street stores that offer maximum style, if not the very best fabric, and make an excellent cost-effective choice. A pale suit is an option but only at a high summer, contemporary wedding. Cream looks better than white and linen or pure cotton are the best fabrics to choose.

Q What about a wedding abroad? Getting married abroad usually involves hot weather, so a traditional dark suit is not the answer. This type of wedding is usually informal so it's fine to think about ditching the jacket and tie and wearing just a shirt and trousers, perhaps with a waistcoat. Look out for cool fabrics such as cotton, silk and linen in light colours like cream and beige.

The stylish groom

Every groom will want to feel confident in his choice of suit and, since his outfit dictates what the rest of the men in the main bridal party will wear, he needs to set the right tone.

Most grooms' attire gets lumped under the label 'formal wear' and he can either buy or, more commonly, hire the whole outfit from the suit to all the accessories. The style of suit is largely dictated by the formality of the wedding.

Morning wear

This is the most popular choice for the groom, traditionally consisting of grey striped trousers, a black, grey or navy single-breasted tailcoat, wing collar shirt, waistcoat, silk tie or cravat and sometimes a top hat. It's a traditional look that suits church and more formal civil ceremonies. Morning wear can be given a more modern look by choosing matching trousers and jacket and the addition of a patterned waistcoat and a plain-collared shirt.

Frock coat

Frock coats are quite a flamboyant look and can be plain, patterned brocade, velvet or silk. They generally reach down to mid-thigh and are worn with a standard or Nehru-style collar. They are worn with plain black trousers, white shirt and cravat and are a modern alternative to morning wear that can be worn at all but the most formal weddings.

Highland dress

Scottish grooms will cut a stylish dash in Highland morning or evening dress, including a kilt, Prince Charlie jacket or doublet, a sporran, laced brogues, socks, bow tie and *sgian dubh* – a small dagger that is worn inside the sock. Other Scottish members of the main bridal party can follow suit.

Military uniform

If your groom is a full-time member of the armed forces, he'll usually wear his uniform to his wedding. If he is an officer, this will be his dress uniform. Asking other guests from the forces to wear their uniform can make for some great photographs.

Lounge suit

At a contemporary, usually civil, wedding, your groom may feel more comfortable wearing a lounge suit. This is his chance to splash out on a designer suit from one of the latest collections. The safest colour choices are black or navy, though cream suits are popular at summer weddings. Team the suit with a new white shirt and a tie to match the theme of the wedding.

Formal wear glossary

Ascot: A wide-neck scarf usually worn with a wing collar that is looped and secured with a tie pin.

Black tie: Also known as a tuxedo. Suitable for a wedding after 5pm.

Buttonhole or boutonniere: A flower that co-ordinates with the wedding colour scheme and is worn on the left lapel by the men in the main bridal party.

Cummerbund: A silk or satin sash worn over the trouser waistband.

Double breasted: A jacket secured with two rows of vertical buttons.

French cuffs: Double cuffs, folded back and worn with cufflinks.

Shawl collar: A jacket lapel with a rounded shape.

Single breasted: A jacket secured with one strip of vertical buttons.

Tails: A formal jacket, worn with white tie, that is short in the front with two longer 'tails' at the back.

White tie: The most formal style, comprising black trousers and jacket, wing-collar shirt and white tie and optional white waistcoat.

Wing collar: A formal dress shirt with stand-up collar, worn with an ascot or bow tie.

Black tie

Black tie is a glamorous choice for a wedding and consists of a dinner jacket, white shirt and black bow tie. It's most suited to a late afternoon ceremony and evening wedding reception in formal surroundings. If the main bridal party is in black tie it follows that the rest of the male guests should wear it too, with the women in evening gowns, and you would usually specify 'black tie' on the invitations.

Groom's accessories

This may be the first time in his life that your groom has had to think about accessories but it's not as daunting as it sounds. The main options include:

Cufflinks: These should suit the formality of a wedding and are available in just about every style and colour imaginable. You can buy personalised cufflinks for a more individual touch, adding the wedding date, the word 'groom' or even a picture of the bride!
Hat: Top hats are not as popular as they once were but if you want to look super-smart it does complete the formal wear style – even though you don't usually wear the topper but just carry it in your left hand. The most usual option would be to hire a hat along with the rest of your outfit.
Jewellery: Most grooms will just wear a watch for their wedding and a wedding band later in the day. Earrings are not to be encouraged.
Shoes: Black shoes are the only option, regardless of the colour of the suit. They should preferably be new and definitely well polished.
Tie: There are three main choices: the standard tie, which can be knotted in different ways depending on the size of the knot you want; the cravat, which is normally worn with morning wear; and the bow tie, usually worn at more formal evening celebrations.
Waistcoat: Usually the groom and his attendants wear matching waistcoats that complement the colour scheme of the wedding. Waistcoats come in lots of different designs and range from the traditional plain to the brightly coloured. It is traditional to leave the bottom button undone.

To buy or hire?

Unless your man goes to lots of weddings and would get the wear out of having his own morning suit, the groom and the rest of the main bridal party are most likely to hire their suits. It's best to organise the hire of the suits at least two months before the big day, particularly if you are marrying in the peak wedding season between June and September when demand for the suits will be high.

Once the groom has chosen the style for his suit and the colour and design for things like the waistcoat and cravat, he needs to let the rest of his groomsmen – and both fathers – know of his choice so they can all arrange for a fitting. Most hire companies will have your suits ready about a week before the wedding so you can have a final fitting and check that everyone has the right size. Don't leave the final fitting until the day before the wedding – there may not be time to make any adjustments. The best man should take charge of ensuring that all the ushers have organised their suits in plenty of time.

Hired outfits are normally returned the first working day after the wedding. This is generally another job for the best man – since the groom will most likely be on his honeymoon. Most hire companies offer an accidental damage waiver, which is definitely worthwhile in case of mishaps, particularly when the drink is flowing!

If your groom decides to buy a suit for his wedding, he should still start looking at least two months in advance so that any fitting adjustments can be made in plenty of time. The groom usually lets other members of the bridal party know what colour suit he will be wearing and the level of formality. If he's wearing a lounge suit, you won't want the fathers and uncles turning up in morning wear.

Groomsmen sizing information

Photocopy this sheet and distribute it to the best man, ushers and fathers if you are hiring their suits.

Contact name

Telephone number

E-mail

Measurements

Height

Usual jacket size

Usual trouser size

Collar size

Waist

Inside leg

Shoe size

Hat size (if required)

Glove size (if required)

Your notes

Formal wear order

If you're hiring outfits, this is the best way to keep track of the order for the groom, best man, ushers and fathers.

Formal wear supplier

Contact

Address

Telephone number

E-mail

Formal wear description (style number/colour)

Date ordered

Date for fitting

Date for return

Groom's outfit	Size ordered	Price
Jacket		£
Trousers		£
Shirt		£
Waistcoat		£
Cummerbund		£
Tie/cravat/bow tie		£
Hat		£
Shoes		£
Total cost		£

Best man's outfit	Size ordered	Price
Jacket		£
Trousers		£
Shirt		£
Waistcoat		£
Cummerbund		£
Tie/cravat/bow tie		£
Hat		£
Shoes		£
Total cost		£

Usher's outfit	Size ordered	Price
Jacket		£
Trousers		£
Shirt		£
Waistcoat		£
Cummerbund		£
Tie/cravat/bow tie		£
Hat		£
Shoes		£
Total cost		£

Father's outfit	Size ordered	Price
Jacket		£
Trousers		£
Shirt		£
Waistcoat		£
Cummerbund		£
Tie/cravat/bow tie		£
Hat		£
Shoes		£
Total cost		£

The beautiful bride

What you'll be wearing is one part of bridal confidence, the other is investing in a beauty regime in the months before the wedding to ensure you look and feel fantastic from top to toe.

The key questions

Q Do you need professional advice? **Anyone, but especially anyone with problem skin, will benefit from a professional facial and nobody blow dries like your hairdresser. Use the appointment to ask the expert all about what products they think will suit you best and how to use them effectively. If you feel stressed, there is nothing like having a neck and shoulder massage at the same time.**

Q How will you wear your hair? **Make an appointment with your hairdresser – or start looking for someone new – about three months before the wedding. Go for a wedding consultation to chat through ideas, ideally taking along your headdress and a picture of your dress so he or she can see the style of your wedding.**

Q What about wedding make-up? **Even if you don't usually wear make-up, you'll need to wear a little if you want to look your best in your photographs. You can book a professional make-up artist or just brave the beauty counters in a department store for pre-wedding advice. Most of the major brands offer a bridal service and they will also give you lots of samples to try at home.**

Q Do you need to diet? **Most brides would like to think they could drop a dress size before their wedding and, if you give yourself a six-month run-up, it is possible. But rather than putting yourself under huge pressure to shed weight, it's better to concentrate on shaping and toning what's already there.**

Q How long will it take to get results? **Realistically you want to allow about three months for a pre-wedding beauty regime. This gives you enough time to see results but not enough time that you'll lose interest or start to feel pressured!**

That sun-kissed look

Most wedding dresses reveal quite a lot of flesh and you'll want that skin to look good. Use lashings of rich moisturiser for a super-soft feel, and boost skin confidence by investing in a light tan. There are lots of DIY fake tanning products but your wedding day isn't the time to chance streaks so a professional tanning treatment is definitely recommended. This can either be applied with a spray gun or by hand and should give a believable result that lasts for anything up to a week – certainly long enough to see you through the wedding and into the first few days of your honeymoon.

Big day make-up essentials

Even if you don't usually wear much make-up, these simple basics should help you get the balance right.

Concealer: Applied under foundation, this is a good idea if you have the odd blemish (but let's hope not!).

All-in-one-foundation and powder: You apply this on a sponge from a compact format. It gives even coverage without adding colour and stops your face from looking shiny.

Blusher: You shouldn't need much blusher – you'll probably have an in-built glow already. For a light blush, use a large blusher brush to sweep a soft rose or peach powder across the top of your cheekbones.

Eyeshadow: A little brown or soft grey eyeshadow lightly smudged across each lid will give your eyes depth and help them to look bigger.

Mascara: Use eyelash curlers before mascara for a real eye-widening effect and – for obvious reasons – use a waterproof mascara. Brown is often more flattering than black for pale complexions.

Lipstick: Choose a soft pink shade with just a hint of glossy shine. Apply one coat, blot, then put on another coat for the longest-lasting effect.

Dressed to Thrill

Your Wedding Gifts

Your Honeymoon

One Week and Counting

Getting stressed out

Weddings are stressful for everyone closely involved but most stressful for the bride. You may well find yourself feeling tired and irritable as the big day approaches – that's perfectly normal! Many brides suffer from what's jokingly referred to as 'the bridezilla syndrome' – a state of mind that overtakes any girl who is planning a wedding, turning her into a bit of a monster!

Don't let stress take hold. You're not superwoman and you can't juggle planning the biggest party of your life, working and having a life without some support. Perhaps your fiancé needs to pull his weight a bit more; it is his wedding too! Delegate some of the less important tasks and get a second opinion if making too many decisions is keeping you awake at night.

And join the *You & Your Wedding* chat room at www.youandyourwedding.co.uk. Thousands of girls are going through the same highs and lows as you are, and who better to talk to than other brides?

Six tips for looking good in wedding photos

1. Never stand square to camera but stand slightly side-on; it will make you look slimmer.
2. If it's hot, take a minute to dab on a little powder before your main photo session so you don't look 'sweaty' in all the shots.
3. Ask to be photographed out of direct sunlight so you don't have to squint. Strong sunlight directly on to your face will also cast dark shadows under your eyes.
4. Tip your chin down as you smile; chin up makes the face look fat.
5. Your smile can quickly look false if you have to keep it up for too long. Every third picture, relax your face and give your mouth a little wiggle before saying 'cheese' again.
6. Hold your bouquet at thigh level. If you hold it too tightly under your bust, you'll look as though you're hiding a baby bump!

Bridal beauty checklist

Appointments you may want to think about in the weeks before the wedding.

Professional facial

Appointment date Time

Eyelash tint

Appointment date Time

Manicure/pedicure

Appointment date Time

Hair cut

Appointment date Time

Hair colour

Appointment date Time

Make-up lesson

Appointment date Time

Professional fake tan

Appointment date Time

Leg wax

Appointment date Time

Bikini wax

Appointment date Time

Your Wedding Gifts

All your friends and family will want to buy you a present in celebration of your marriage and you'll want to say thanks to those who have helped to make your big day possible. So where do you start?

The key questions

Q Do you really need a gift list? Making a list of items you want people to buy just because you are getting married is an embarrassing concept for many couples, especially those who already have a home together. But most people will want to buy you something and, unless you give them some clues as to what you want, you will get presents you don't want and they will have wasted time and money.

Q Where do you go to register? You have several options, from the major department stores to specialist gift list companies that can source just about anything from the traditional to the unusual. None of the services charge you for managing the list and since many have an online service it's a simple process for both you and your guests.

Q What sort of gifts should you choose? Put together a list with a wide variety of gift options and prices to suit individuals as well as groups of people, such as work mates who may want to join together and buy a larger gift. Traditional wedding list items are china, cutlery, glasses, linens and kitchen electricals but you can also choose a more specialised list such as one from a garden centre. Store vouchers are a modern addition to many gift lists allowing the couple of buy items at leisure.

Q Can you ask for cash instead? **Asking for cash is a tricky one. It used to be considered bad manners but these days many of your friends may appreciate that you just don't need anything for your home and that cash would be useful to spend at a later date. It's always better to suggest that you are saving towards a specific item, like a conservatory or new kitchen, so people know what the money will be going towards. If it's all too awkward, suggest store vouchers instead, which many people don't see as cash.**

Q Who do you need to thank? **Apart from gifts you receive you also need to think about presents to give to key members of the bridal party for all their help in the run-up to the wedding. That includes the best man, bridesmaids and both sets of parents.**

A wedding gift list

A wedding list is just that – a list of items you'd like to receive if people are feeling generous enough to buy them for you. It can be arranged through a department store, a specialist gift list shop, online or you can do it yourself.

The list is usually sorted three to four months before the wedding, sooner if you like, though details of the what, when and how need to be finalised by the time you send out your invitations. You should compile your list with your fiancé; shopping may not be his idea of fun but the items you choose are for you both, so you'll want to choose them together.

Before you start looking for specifics, try to make out a rough list of what you actually need. Gift list basics are linens, china, cutlery, towels, small electrical appliances, tools, picture frames and decorative ornaments. This is your chance to replace older items and treat yourselves to the latest designer gadgets.

If you already have all the basics you need, there's nothing to say you can't broaden the present spectrum a bit and include sporting items, gym equipment and things for the garden. But do try to stick to items that your guests, and particularly the more traditional-minded ones, will think are suitable for a wedding.

It's worth checking out the possible gift list options before picking which one to use. The service offered by various department stores will differ and the brands they stock may not be the same. This is where the internet will come in very handy. Log on to the various shops and read through the gift registry section. At the same time look through what they stock and the patterns for things like china and cutlery so you won't be disappointed.

Now ask yourself the following questions about each list provider:

- How is the list managed? The online services give the most flexibility for you and your guests.
- Can your guests order items online, over the phone and in person? Can they use credit cards?
- When are the gifts sent out? Some ship all in one go after the wedding: others send individual gifts as soon as they are bought.
- Will items ordered months before the wedding actually be in stock after the big day when it's time for delivery, or will there be a long wait?
- Is there a charge for delivery?
- Does the company offer gift-wrapping?
- What is the returns policy if you don't like something or change your mind after the wedding?
- Is there a deadline for when all gifts must be delivered after the wedding?
- How long will your list remain open?

Your gift list choices

You have several choices when it comes to managing your gifts, depending on what you want. Each has plus points, so do your research to find which suits you the best.

A department store

This is the easiest and most obvious place to put your gift list. They are all managed much the same, though the ones with an online facility will make life easier for your guests because they can see what they are buying and can usually order online and pay with a credit card. You'll be able to check your list online too, tracking what has been bought and whether you need to add more if you are proving popular!

Most stores have an in-store adviser who will show you what to do. You either get a clipboard and paper to walk around the shop jotting down the make, price and stock number of anything that takes your fancy or use a hand-held scanner to simply zap the item barcode. All your chosen goodies are then put on to one master list with your names and wedding date.

The master list is held at the store and is updated regularly as guests make their purchases. Your gift list adviser will send you updates as well so you can see who has bought each gift.

Once your list is sorted, the store will probably give you a pack of branded gift registration cards that state '*Kate and Chris have their gift list at .... store*', with contact details and a reference number. You can either pop one of these in with your invitations or wait until someone asks for your list details and then hand one over.

A gift list company

This type of company is dedicated just to wedding lists and you get a very personal service from goodies such as a glass of wine when you compile your list to online back-up. It usually offers a much wider selection of items than a department store and they can source more unusual, and expensive, designer brands.

The management of the list is much the same as with a department store and you'll get regular updates of how the list is progressing. Most specialist companies have a website facility so guests can see what they are buying. They usually make one delivery of all your gifts on an agreed date once the list is closed.

Doing it yourself

If you have a computer and a willing mum or friend who wants to take charge, you may decide on the do-it-yourself option, giving you maximum flexibility to choose a wide range of items from a wide range of shops.

The master list needs to be held by one willing and organised person who is available to send out copies to anyone who asks, answer questions and make a note of items as gifts are chosen.

The main problem with a DIY list is knowing when items have been bought since you'll need to rely on guests either telling you they've bought something or finding out when it's delivered. The chance of duplicate gifts is high but most shops have a refund or exchange policy so this may not be a problem.

Consider the unusual

If you already have pretty much everything you need, you may like to have a list where guests pledge money towards something, such as your honeymoon. Several of the major tour operators now offer 'honey money' where guests can put cash into a fund for you to spend on spa treatments, boat trips or even towards the cost of the trip itself. Or how about creating a new garden for your home? Garden centre gift lists allow guests to pledge money towards gardening equipment, trees and plants – sometimes a design service or even a conservatory.

Some couples like to have a charity gift list, so guests pledge a donation to a major charity, such as Oxfam, or choose from a selection of items for use in developing countries. How good will it make you and your guests feel to think your day has provided fresh water for a village or school books for several children?

Present problems

Even if you have a wedding gift list, you are bound to receive a few things you don't want and you'll need to handle the situation with care if you want to avoid hurt feelings.

You hate the present: Having a gift list doesn't guarantee that one of your guests won't go 'off list' and give you a gift of their own choosing that you hate. If the giver is a close relative or friend who's likely to be a regular visitor, accept that you're going to have to keep their gift, albeit hidden in a cupboard to be taken out again every time they visit! If they are unlikely to be in your home very often and you know where the item was bought, ask to exchange it. Providing it's still boxed, there shouldn't be a problem.

The gift is broken: If something you receive from your gift list supplier arrives broken, call the shop and tell them as soon as it arrives and ask for a replacement. If the gift was given on the wedding day, try to find out subtly if the giver used a credit card, in which case the card insurance should cover the damage and it can be replaced.

Duplicate gifts: You may need more than one set of sheets or towels but perhaps not two or three toasters! Exchange goods at department stores and your guests need never know.

Saying thank you

You'll want to say a personal and sincere thank you to everyone who has come to your wedding and generously given you a gift. And a written thank you is expected even if you said thanks in person at the wedding.

Writing out a hundred plus thank-you cards is time consuming and it's a job that both you and your groom should tackle together. The easiest way is for you to thank your friends and family and for him to do the same. Split joint friends between both of you.

Send out thank yous as soon as you can after you have received the gift. If presents arrive before the wedding, you can send a thank you straight away.

If you do leave your thank-you notes until after the wedding, make sure you send them within four weeks; any longer and you run the risk of being considered rude.

You should handwrite your thank-you cards – you don't need to be told that e-mails or photocopied sheets are impolite! You can order cards with the same design as your invitations or buy packs of thank-you cards from any high street stationer.

Nobody expects a literary masterpiece – they simply want to know that you appreciated their gift and their company at the wedding. Personalise each card by mentioning the gift and perhaps saying something about how you may use it in the future. For example: 'Thank you so much for the fabulous toaster. I will think of you every morning when Michael serves me breakfast in bed!' If someone has given you money, try to give an idea of how the money may be spent, even if you have yet to decide.

Wedding gift list checklist

A checklist of wedding list favourites to help you before you start shopping.

	Make/pattern	Quantity	Price
Kitchen items			
Bin			£
Blender			£
Cheese board			£
Cheese grater			£
Coffee maker			£
Food processor			£
Frying pans			£
Hand mixer			£
Ice-cream maker			£
Kettle			£
Knife block			£
Microwave			£
Mixing bowls			£
Mugs			£
Saucepans			£
Toaster			£
Wok			£
Other			£
Dining items			
Coffee cups			£
Coffee pot			£
Cutlery			£
Everyday dinner service			
● dinner plates			£
● small plates			£
● soup/cereal bowls			£

	Make/pattern	Quantity	Price
Formal dinner service			
● chargers			£
● dinner plates			£
● small plates			£
● soup bowls			£
● dessert bowls			£
Napkins			£
Placemats			£
Salad bowl			£
Table cloth			£
Tea service			£
Other			£
Glasses			
Champagne flutes			£
Red wine goblets			£
Tumblers			
● short			£
● tall			£
White wine glasses			£
Other			£
Bed linens			
Blankets			£
Duvet			£
Duvet cover			£
Pillows			£
Pillowcases			£
Sheets			£
Throw			£
Other			£

	Make/pattern	Quantity	Price
Bathroom			
Bath mat			£
Bath towels			£
Beach towels			£
Guest towels			£
Hand towels			£
Other			£
General			
CD player			£
Computer			£
Dishwasher			£
DVD player			£
Garden furniture			£
Garden tools			£
iPod			£
Lawn mower			£
Picture frames			£
Pictures			£
Radio			£
Telephone			£
Television			£
Vases			£
Washing machine/dryer			£
Other			£

Gifts received

This will help you to track the presents you have received and make sure a thank-you note is sent.

Name of guest	Gift received	Date received	Thank-you sent

Name of guest	Gift received	Date received	Thank-you sent

Gifts from the bride and groom

Key questions

Q Who should receive a present? **A wedding takes lots of organisation and it's nice to thank those who helped make it all come together with a gift for all their hard work. You may also like to thank anyone who contributed at the ceremony giving a reading or musical performance.**

Q How much should you spend? **You don't have to spend a fortune but the present should be something appropriate to each person. It is usual to spend a little more on the chief bridesmaid and best man and it's always best to choose gifts, like jewellery, that can be kept as a treasured reminder of your day.**

Q When do you give the gifts? **The groom traditionally presents the gifts as part of his speech at the reception. The bride is usually involved as well when it comes to handing out the gifts to both your mums and anyone like a soloist or the wedding planner.**

Chief bridesmaid

She is likely to be your sister or best friend and to have been invaluable in the run-up to the wedding and on the day so she deserves a well-chosen gift.
Ideas: A necklace, earrings, a bracelet, a watch, a designer handbag, an iPod, a spa day.

Best man

Like the chief bridesmaid, the best man will probably have been most involved in the wedding preparations and deserves a good thank you.
Ideas: Designer cufflinks, a leather wallet, shares in his favourite football club, a case of wine or champagne.

Adult bridesmaids

Many brides pay for their bridesmaids' outfits and consider this thanks enough, but it's still polite to make a small gesture on the wedding day. To avoid any potentially ruffled feathers, it's best to give the same gift to them all.

Ideas: A charm bracelet, earrings, a voucher for a beauty treatment, designer perfume.

Younger bridesmaids and page boys

Apart from paying for their outfits, your youngest attendants will love the chance to come up to receive a gift from the groom at the reception.

Ideas: A teddy, a charm bracelet, a children's CD player, a train set, a Gameboy.

Ushers

The ushers don't play a huge role in the wedding but still deserve a thank you from the bride and groom for their time and effort.

Ideas: A money clip, designer cufflinks, a tankard engraved with the wedding date.

Mothers of the bride/groom

Your mothers will probably have done a great deal of work in the run-up to the wedding and it's traditional to present them both with a large bouquet or flower arrangement. Another nice idea is to arrange for a gift to be sent to each set of parents a day or two after the wedding when you're away on your honeymoon. A tree for the garden or a framed print from the wedding delivered with a hand-written note from you both is a lovely idea.

Thank-you gifts

All your attendants will appreciate a present for their hard work before and at the wedding.

	Gift	Cost
Chief bridesmaid		£
Bridesmaid 1		£
Bridesmaid 2		£
Bridesmaid 3		£
Flower girl 1		£
Flower girl 2		£
Page boy		£
Best man		£
Usher 1		£
Usher 2		£
Usher 3		£
Mother of bride		£
Mother of groom		£
Other		£
Total gift budget		£

Your Honeymoon

The world's your oyster when it comes to booking the perfect honeymoon. And this once-in-a-lifetime holiday needs careful planning if you want to enjoy every romantic moment to the full.

The key questions

Q Where in the world? This is your chance to experience somewhere you've never visited before. It needs to be a destination you both want to visit and have all the elements to fulfil your requirements, such as a top-quality resort, great sightseeing, sporting activities, shopping and good restaurants.

Q What kind of trip? It's important that it's a trip you'll both enjoy. Spend some time before booking talking about what you both want from the honeymoon. How important is a good beach? A mixture of activities? Good nightlife? If you can't agree on one destination, maybe you should be thinking about a two-centre trip that combines both your requirements.

Q How long should you be away? The average honeymoon is two weeks; any less and you probably won't feel properly relaxed and refreshed after all the stresses of the wedding. But if money is tight you might like to splurge on a great hotel for a shorter trip (being spoiled rotten helps you to relax faster!) and promise yourselves a second – longer – honeymoon at a later date.

Q What is your budget? The honeymoon is usually part of the wedding budget so you need to set aside a realistic amount.

Do lots of research with travel agents and independently using websites to see what deals are available. Being flexible on dates, for example, and not flying at peak times can save you lots of money.

You should allow plenty of time to arrange this all-important holiday; booking about six months in advance is usual. It sounds obvious, but check that both your passports are valid for the duration of the trip and for six months beyond. If you need a new passport, apply well in advance; the Passport Office gets very busy during traditional holiday times and you need to allow for any delays.

If you plan to change your surname and want to travel in your newly married name, you need to get your passport changed before the trip. You can do this up to three months before the wedding, though you won't be able to use the new passport until after you are married. Check out the Passport Office website for more details (www.passport.gov.uk/passport_amending_marriage.asp). Remember that your travel documents and your passport must be in the same name. You can travel in your maiden name (even if you'll be changing your name later on) but all documents must match.

Making the decision

You need to be realistic about your honeymoon budget. The UK average honeymoon costs about £3,000 but you can spend less – or a lot more! Enjoy an indulgent evening with a pile of brochures and surf the internet to compare prices.

Who decides on the destination?

Traditionally, the groom surprised his bride by choosing the honeymoon destination and keeping it a secret until the last minute. Fine if you trust his judgement but it's probably safer to drop some heavy hints about what constitutes your dream trip, just in case!

What do you want from your honeymoon?

- ❒ Stay in the UK
- ❒ Short haul (maximum 4 hours' flying time)
- ❒ Long haul (over 4 hours' flying time)
- ❒ Warm weather
- ❒ Beach
- ❒ Diving
- ❒ Sporting activities
- ❒ City
- ❒ Culture
- ❒ Nightlife
- ❒ Adventure
- ❒ Winter sports
- ❒ A cruise
- ❒ Two centres

Prioritise what matters to the two of you. For some a buzzy resort with lots to do is a must: for others seclusion and quiet is what appeals. Of course, you may not want the same thing from a holiday, in which case a two-centre trip may be the answer, with action to start and relaxation to finish.

Stretching your honeymoon budget

Shop around: Ask at least three different tour operators for their best price – you'll be amazed at what you can save on the same trip. Include a Saturday night in your package to get the best air fares.

Get web-savvy: Use the internet for best deals; you'll often find more choice and booking online may save you at least 10 per cent.

Be flexible: Try to travel at off-peak times. This is not an option during the summer but do ask, for example, about flying on a Monday or Tuesday rather than at the more popular weekend.

Travel smart: Flight upgrades aren't usually forthcoming but you'll stand a much better chance if you are smartly dressed and look as though you belong in the first class lounge.

Indulge yourselves: It's your honeymoon so up the luxury factor by staying fewer nights but in a fabulous hotel.

The all-inclusive option: If you enjoy sports, check out all-inclusive packages where a lot of activities are included in the one price, as well as most food and drinks.

Tell the world: Let everyone know you are on your honeymoon – at the airport, in hotels, in restaurants. You never know what freebies may come your way!

Ask the experts

If you are not experienced travellers, it's as well to ask the experts about anything that could potentially spoil your trip. If you are using a tour operator or travel agent, take advantage of their expertise. If you are arranging the trip independently, check tourist board websites and accommodation details direct with the hotel.

- Is the area safe? Are there places we should avoid, particularly at night?
- Can we drink the water and eat all local food safely?
- Do we need inoculations or other health precautions?
- Are flights direct (stopovers can be exhausting)?
- What's the local currency?
- What's the local voltage (so you can use your hairdryer, toothbrush, shaver and so on)?
- Do you recommend a hire car to get around?
- Can we request a special in-flight meal?
- Can we pre-book our seats?
- Are hotel transfers included in the price?
- Is there a special honeymoon package at the hotel?

- Can we request a special room such as the honeymoon suite or arrange to have a sea view?

Safety first

Find out what inoculations you need at www.netdoctor.co.uk or pick up a Department of Health E111 leaflet from your GP. To discover if a destination is safe to visit, check the Foreign Office website at www.fco.gov.uk. And make sure you take out travel insurance before you go.

Pain-free packing tips

Less is more: You really don't need to pack masses of clothes for any trip and piles of luggage will just add to your stress levels. Research the destination: look on the internet and read up on where you are visiting. Check out the latest weather forecast and find out if the hotel has a dress code for dinner.

Make a list: Lists are always useful and will help to make sure you don't miss anything. If it ends up as a hugely long list, it may also focus your mind on what to cut out!

Pack smart: Put heavy items at the bottom of the case and the things you know you'll need first at the top. Decant beauty and hair products into smaller plastic bottles and wrap anything that may leak in plastic bags – there's nothing worse than sticky luggage on arrival.

Half and half: Put half of your clothes into one case with half of his clothes and the rest into another case. If you're unlucky enough to lose one case on route, at least you'll both have something to wear when you arrive.

Ten favourite honeymoon destinations

1. Antigua
2. Barbados
3. Florida
4. Greece
5. Italy
6. Jamaica
7. The Maldives
8. Mauritius
9. South Africa
10. Thailand

Hand luggage essentials

Depending on the current rules and regulations about what you can carry on to the plane, this is the ideal list of what you'll want to keep with you at all times.

- ❒ Passport, visa and other form of identification such as a driving licence
- ❒ Tickets
- ❒ Hotel confirmation
- ❒ Local currency for tips and taxis on arrival
- ❒ Travellers' cheques
- ❒ Prescription medication
- ❒ Glasses, contact lenses
- ❒ Valuable jewellery
- ❒ Camera
- ❒ House and car keys
- ❒ Moisturiser, wet wipes, toothbrush and toothpaste
- ❒ A basic change of light clothing (t-shirt, shorts, underwear)

Don't leave home without them

- ❒ Prescription medicine
- ❒ Pain relief such as paracetamol
- ❒ Antiseptic and antihistamine creams
- ❒ Birth control
- ❒ A spare pair of glasses/contact lenses
- ❒ A mini first aid kit with plasters
- ❒ Insect repellent
- ❒ Diarrhoea medicine
- ❒ Sunscreen
- ❒ Aftersun lotion
- ❒ Antacid tablets

Packing suggestions for a stylish honeymoon

Bride

- ❑ 1 jacket
- ❑ 1 cardigan
- ❑ 2 pairs of jeans/casual trousers
- ❑ 2 pairs of shorts/cropped trousers
- ❑ 5 casual tops/vests
- ❑ 2 sundresses
- ❑ 3 evening outfits
- ❑ 2 swimsuits/bikinis
- ❑ Underwear
- ❑ Socks
- ❑ Nightdress
- ❑ Casual sandals
- ❑ Dressy sandals
- ❑ Flip-flops
- ❑ Trainers

Optional extras

- ❑ Sunhat
- ❑ Workout clothes
- ❑ Beach cover up
- ❑ Beach bag
- ❑ Evening wrap
- ❑ Evening bag
- ❑ Fold-up umbrella
- ❑ Hairdryer
- ❑ Adaptor

Groom

- ❑ 1 jacket
- ❑ 1 sweater/sweatshirt
- ❑ 2 pairs of jeans/casual trousers
- ❑ 2 pairs of shorts
- ❑ 5 casual shirts/t-shirts
- ❑ 2 smart short-sleeved shirts
- ❑ 3 dress shirts/optional ties
- ❑ 2 pairs of swimming shorts
- ❑ Underwear
- ❑ Socks
- ❑ Pyjamas
- ❑ Deck shoes
- ❑ Dress shoes
- ❑ Flip-flops
- ❑ Trainers

Optional extras

- ❑ Sunhat
- ❑ Workout clothes
- ❑ Golf clothes

Your notes

Two-centre honeymoons

You like lazing on the beach but your man wants action and adventure: you want big-city buzz and he wants relaxation and quiet. Well, they say opposites attract and choosing your honeymoon destination could be the first test of compromise in your marriage.

Two-centre holidays are already popular and make the perfect honeymoon, usually combining two very different places so you feel you are getting two holidays for the price of one. Here are some well-balanced suggestions:

Action	Relaxation
Big game African Safari	Flopping on a Mauritian beach
Skiing at Lake Tahoe, USA	Chilling in Las Vegas
Shopping in Miami	Driving through the Florida Keys
The sights of Sydney	The beaches in Queensland
Clubbing in London	Log fires in the Cotswolds
A walking tour of Paris	A secluded Normandy château
Shopping and football in Madrid	The beaches of Marbella

A happy honeymoon

You are bound to have romantic expectations about your honeymoon – sun, sea and lots of sex – but don't expect it to be hearts and flowers every minute of the trip; that is just not real life and you don't want to suffer from the honeymoon blues.

It probably isn't your first time travelling together so you'll have a pretty good idea of whether your partner is a good traveller or not. Make allowances for the fact that you'll both be tired and, having just experienced the biggest event of your lives, you may feel a little low once you reach the calm of the honeymoon suite.

The first couple of days of the trip are a good time to chat about all the wedding details, the highs and lows, which bit you both enjoyed the most and what didn't go quite according to plan. Once this is done, try not to talk about the wedding again. You have lived and breathed your big day for long enough and there is no going back, so aim to put it all behind you – at least until you get home and see the wedding photographs!

Indulge each other with little surprises, take advantage of all the honeymoon extras that will probably come your way such as a candlelit dinner, a romantic cruise, spa treatments for two. Simply revel in your newly married status. But don't feel you have to spend every waking moment in each other's company. If either of you wants to go for a run, a swim or a walk on the beach alone, that's fine. Being married doesn't mean being together all the time and you are allowed to be independent during some of the honeymoon.

A honeymoon is so much more than a holiday and you'll want to remember every minute so think about putting together a honeymoon diary or scrapbook. Include a selection of photos, your travel tickets and matchbooks from each of the romantic restaurants you visit. Write down names of favourite places visited, what music was playing and what you ate. It is amazing how quickly you can forget little details, and your honeymoon is one trip you won't want to forget in a hurry.

The world's 10 best beaches

- Maundays Bay, Anguilla
- Jumby Bay Beach, Antigua
- Pink Sands, Bahamas
- Matira Beach, Bora Bora
- Woolacombe, Cornwall
- Wilson Island, Great Barrier Reef, Australia
- Datai Beach, Langkawi, Malaysia
- Le Morne Peninsula, Mauritius
- Maroma Beach, Mexico
- Denis Island, Seychelles

One Week and Counting

The big day has nearly arrived. The week before the wedding is when all of your hard work comes together and hopefully by now you are so organised nothing important will be forgotten. Enjoy it!

The key questions

Q What's still to be done? **It's all about the details now, making sure everyone knows what's happening and when. Final numbers need to be confirmed to the venue, if this hasn't been done already. And it's a good idea to double check with all suppliers (florist, transport provider, photographer and so on) that everything is as you expect.**

Q Have you have forgotten anything? **Chances are you haven't, but just in case read through all your planning notes one last time. Sit down with your fiancé and chat through every element of the wedding day, from start to finish, to ensure it's all covered.**

Q Who still needs to be paid? **The week before the wedding is the time to make all your final payments. Once numbers are confirmed, the caterers will expect to be paid (and you won't be able to change numbers after this is done). On the day, your groom will need to remember cash for tips and any unforeseen little extras.**

Q Are you suffering from last-minute nerves? **You are quite likely to be feeling some last-minute jitters but relax – it's quite normal.**

You have been planning this day for such a long time and the big moment has nearly arrived. You want to enjoy the day so try to keep a sense of perspective; if the odd thing doesn't go quite to plan, so what? You are marrying the man you love!

The week before your wedding is bound to be an exciting time, with lots going on and masses still to think about. If possible, book a few days off work so you can really enjoy the build-up to the big day as well as planning a few last-minute pampering treats.

Last-minute checklist

A week before the wedding make some phone calls – and follow up with an e-mail if necessary – to everyone who is involved to double check roles, responsibilities and timings.

The key players

- ❒ Officiant
- ❒ Best man
- ❒ Bridesmaid(s)
- ❒ Ushers
- ❒ Flower girl(s)
- ❒ Page boy
- ❒ Ceremony readers
- ❒ Ceremony soloists
- ❒ Others

Your suppliers

- ❒ Caterer
- ❒ Venue
- ❒ Florist
- ❒ Photographer
- ❒ Videographer
- ❒ DJ/band

- ❒ Entertainers
- ❒ Transport provider
- ❒ Cake maker
- ❒ First night hotel
- ❒ Travel agent
- ❒ Others

Last-minute tasks for the bride and/or groom

- ❒ Collect the wedding dress
- ❒ Collect any hired outfits
- ❒ Collect the wedding rings
- ❒ Run through the vows
- ❒ Practise the reception speeches
- ❒ Collect travellers' cheques and currency
- ❒ Pack for the honeymoon
- ❒ Give a play list to the DJ/band
- ❒ Give a shot list to the photographer
- ❒ Put a welcome pack into the rooms of out-of-town guests
- ❒ Wrap all thank-you gifts
- ❒ Have a hair cut or trim and a conditioning treatment
- ❒ Have a manicure and pedicure
- ❒ Have a fake tanning treatment
- ❒ Enjoy a romantic dinner together

Wedding day essentials

Little things every bride will want to have close to hand

- tissues
- pain relief
- hair pins
- clear nail polish
- mobile phone
- lipstick, compact, comb, hairspray
- safety pins
- nail file
- breath mints
- plasters

The hen and stag night

You may have already held your hen night, and you certainly shouldn't leave this celebration until the last minute, but the weekend before the wedding is a popular date to enjoy a party with your girlfriends and for your groom to hold his stag night.

The chief bridesmaid and the best man usually shoulder the main task of arranging something that each of you will enjoy so, if you have firm ideas of what you would and wouldn't like to do, make sure you let them know in plenty of time.

Who to invite?

The guest list for a hen night should include bridesmaids, the bride's closest friends and relatives and usually the groom's closest female relatives as well. Whether to invite both mothers is really up to you and what you are planning to do. If the hen event isn't the sort of thing your mothers will enjoy you can always plan a nice lunch so they won't feel left out of the girly goings-on.

For a stag night, it's usually the best man, ushers and the groom's closest friends and relatives. In either case, only people invited to the wedding should be invited to this evening out.

When and where?

The when can be anything up to about a month before the wedding, depending on when everyone is free to come along. The where offers you lots of choice and certainly doesn't just mean drinking too much and making a fool of yourself! These days you can do anything from pole dancing classes to making a pop video. Think about the mix of people you'll be inviting; it's much better to match the event to the people rather than the other way round. And keep the cost in mind; not everyone earns the same amount of money and you don't want people having to miss the evening because your idea is too expensive.

Who pays?

The hen or stag is traditionally not expected to contribute towards their own hen/stag night, unless it involves something pricey such as staying in a hotel or flying abroad.

Each of the guests usually adds 10 per cent of the proposed cost of the evening to a kitty and this pays for the bride- or groom-to-be and saves them having to buy a drink all evening.

Some favourite hen night ideas:

- a pampering spa day/weekend
- visiting a comedy club
- making a pop video (and showing it at the wedding)
- a European shopping day/weekend
- a weekend in New York
- a chocoholics cookery class
- driving a fast car (or even a tank) around a track
- disco-hopping in a limo
- a slumber party in a fancy hotel

Some favourite stag night ideas:

- a meal followed by bar hopping
- a golf day/weekend
- going to see Real Madrid/Barcelona play
- driving a fast car (or even a tank) around a track
- visiting a comedy club
- paint balling
- horse/greyhound racing
- a poker night
- a weekend in New York
- a weekend in Amsterdam
- go-karting

Hen or stag night organiser's checklist

- ❑ In consultation with the bride- or groom-to-be, make a list of guests.
- ❑ Come up with an event idea and date when most people seem free.
- ❑ Plan an itinerary and book everything in advance so you are sure to get in. Pay any deposits and ensure you know who has/hasn't paid.
- ❑ Send out invitations mentioning the date, timings and expected cost.
- ❑ To liven up the evening, ask guests to bring along old photographs, props and so on – anything that will make a good story about the hen or stag in their younger days.
- ❑ Pre-book everything for the evening, making sure that any venues are happy to accommodate a large single-sex group (many are not).
- ❑ Plan everything down to the last detail and make sure everyone has your mobile number; it's easy to get separated if you are moving from one place to another.
- ❑ Arrange transport home (for you and the bride/groom if no one else!).

The wedding rehearsal

If it will help to calm your nerves you may like to arrange a ceremony rehearsal to run through all the major elements of what will happen. A rehearsal is by no means essential but, particularly if you are having a large wedding with lots of different elements, it can be very useful. Speak to your vicar or registrar to see if it's possible to arrange this for a day or two before the wedding. It means bringing together all the key players – or suitable stand-ins if necessary – and you literally run through the ceremony from the minute you walk down the aisle.

It's a great opportunity for everyone to perfect their roles. The ushers will know the layout of the venue and see the seating arrangements, readers can practise their words and you'll get a chance to run through your vows.

A wedding rehearsal is usually followed by an informal lunch or dinner for everyone involved. It's a nice start to the celebrations and will help everyone get to know one another better.

The wedding day countdown

First thing…	The bride should have a good breakfast; she will be too excited to eat much later on. Finish packing for the honeymoon. The bride has a relaxing bath.
3–4 hours to go…	Bride's hair and make-up. If she is having her hair done at a salon, allow at least 2 hours. Bridesmaids and mothers also get their hair and make-up done. Bouquet and buttonholes are either delivered or collected.
2 hours to go…	Bride departs for the civil venue (if changing there) or starts to get dressed with her mother and maids. Groom and best man get dressed and ready.
1 hour to go…	Parents and bridesmaids gather for family photographs with the bride.
30 minutes to go…	Ushers greet guests at the ceremony venue, giving each one the order of service and showing them to their seats. Remember – bride's family to the left, groom's to the right.
20 minutes to go…	Groom and best man arrive at the ceremony. Prelude music begins.
10 minutes to go…	Bridesmaids, bride's mother/groom's parents arrive.
5 minutes to go…	The groom/best man take their position at the altar. The bride's mother and groom's parents take their seats at the front of the ceremony. The officiant takes his/her place.
Ceremony begins…	The processional music starts and the bride and her father, followed (or preceded) by the bridesmaids walk up the aisle. The guests rise to greet the bride. The ceremony begins.

What happens if…

The chances are everything will go according to plan but, just in case, here are some handy hints for dealing with the unexpected.

… I break out in spots? If you feel a spot threatening to erupt the day before the wedding, lessen the redness by putting a blob of toothpaste on it overnight. A dab of witch hazel followed by concealer and then powder will help to make it a lot less obvious. Don't squeeze whatever you do!

… it rains? Don't let rain spoil any part of your day. Invest in several extra-large white umbrellas to keep close to hand at each of the venues. Always expect a downpour, even in the summer, by having a Plan B for your terrace drinks reception and check that any marquee is weatherproofed.

… it's boiling hot? The heat can be more of a problem than rain. Make sure you have shade for your guests, particularly while they are waiting around during photographs, and that there is plenty of water to drink.

… my dress gets dirty? Ask your dress shop for tips on the best way to clean any marks or repair any minor problems like a fallen hem or hole in the seams. White chalk is often the best way to cover minor marks.

… my car gets stuck in traffic or breaks down? It's the stuff of nightmares and hopefully the car company will have allowed for such eventualities. But just in case, have a friend with a smart car standing by to step in.

… one of us feels faint at the altar? This happens more often than you think. The combination of lack of food and extreme nerves can take their toll. Tell someone how you feel, and sit with your head down until you recover.

… there is a problem at the reception? If there's a glitch with the food and everything is running a bit late, try not to worry. You are probably the only ones who will notice. If the seating plan needs a last-minute tweak, leave it to the banqueting manager to add/move a chair or two. If excess alcohol means a couple of guests are behaving badly, leave it to the best man and ushers to sort out – it's one of the reasons they are there.

Now all that's left is for you to have a wonderful – and very well organised – wedding day. Good luck and enjoy every single minute!

Master list of contacts

Complete these details for all your suppliers and keep them close to hand during the final week.

	Name	Contact number(s)	E-mail
Minister/registrar			
Wedding planner			
Dress designer			
Venue			
Venue manager			
Caterer			
Cake maker			
Photographer			
Videographer			
Florist			
Stationers			
DJ/band			
Entertainer			
Transport			
Hairdresser			
Make-up artist			
First night hotel			
Travel agent			
Other			

Your notes

General wedding appointments

Use these sheets to track appointments with the venue, for dress fittings and any wedding suppliers.

Appointment 1

Name of shop/supplier

Contact name

Contact number

Date/time

Your notes

Appointment 2

Name of shop/supplier

Contact name

Contact number

Date/time

Your notes

Appointment 3

Name of shop/supplier

Contact name

Contact number

Date/time

Your notes

Appointment 4

Name of shop/supplier

Contact name

Contact number

Date/time

Your notes

Appointment 5

Name of shop/supplier

Contact name

Contact number

Date/time

Your notes

Appointment 6

Name of shop/supplier

Contact name

Contact number

Date/time

Your notes

Appointment 7

Name of shop/supplier

Contact name

Contact number

Date/time

Your notes

Appointment 8

Name of shop/supplier

Contact name

Contact number

Date/time

Your notes

Appointment 9

Name of shop/supplier

Contact name

Contact number

Date/time

Your notes

Appointment 10

Name of shop/supplier

Contact name

Contact number

Date/time

Your notes

Appointment 11

Name of shop/supplier

Contact name

Contact number

Date/time

Your notes

Appointment 12

Name of shop/supplier

Contact name

Contact number

Date/time

Your notes

Appointment 13

Name of shop/supplier

Contact name

Contact number

Date/time

Your notes

Appointment 14

Name of shop/supplier

Contact name

Contact number

Date/time

Your notes

Appointment 15

Name of shop/supplier

Contact name

Contact number

Date/time

Your notes

Appointment 16

Name of shop/supplier

Contact name

Contact number

Date/time

Your notes

Your Wedding Address Book

www.youandyourwedding.co.uk is the perfect wedding website, whether you want to work out your budget, find great suppliers or just talk to other brides in the chat room, you'll find it all there.

Accessories

Angela Hale Jewellery
www.angela-hale.co.uk

Butler & Wilson
www.butlerandwilson.co.uk

Cavendish French
01372 459944

Christian Louboutin
www.christianlouboutin.fr

Coleman Douglas Pearls
020 7373 3369
www.astleyclarke.com

Dominic Walmsley Jewellery
020 7250 0125
www.dominicwalmsley.com

Dower & Hall
020 7589 8474

Filippa Scott
www.filippascott.com

Gina
020 7409 7090

Halo Headdresses
01694 771470
www.shropshirebrides.co.uk

Jimmy Choo Shoes
www.jimmychoo.com

Katz Bridal Shoes
www.ktbridal.co.uk

Katzi Jewellery
www.katzi.co.uk

Leigh-Anne McCague
www.leigh-annemccaguetiaras.com

Petals International
www.petals-international.co.uk

Polly Edwards Tiaras
www.pollyedwards.com

Rainbow Club Shoes
www.rainbowclub.co.uk

Van Peterson Designs
www.vanpeterson.com

Wright & Teague
www.wrightandteague.co.uk

Cake makers

Celebration Cakes
01189 424581
www.celebcakes.com

Choccywoccydoodah
01273 329462
www.choccywoccydoodah.com

Contemporary Cake Designs
www.contemporarycakedesigns.com

Konditor & Cook
020 7261 0456
www.konditorandcook.com

Linda Fripp
01722 718518
www.lindafrippcakes.co.uk

The Little Venice Cake Company
020 7486 5252
www.lvcc.co.uk

Lola's Kitchen
0845 052 369

Pat-a-Cake-Pat-a-Cake
020 7485 0006

Peggy Porschen
www.peggyporschen.com

Purita Hyam
01403 891518
www.chocolateweddingcakes.co.uk

Rachel Mount Cakes
020 8672 9333
www.rachelmount.com

Savoir Design
020 8788 0808
www.savoirdesign.com

Tina K
020 8883 9862

Catering companies

Admirable Crichton
020 7326 3800
www.admirable-crichton.co.uk

Blistering Barbecues
020 7720 7678
www.blistering.co.uk

Bovingdons
020 8874 8032
www.bovingdons.co.uk

Create Food
01883 625905
www.createfood.co.uk

Jalapeno
020 7639 6500
www.jalapenolondon.co.uk

Tapenade
www.tapenade.co.uk

Urban Caprice
www.urbancaprice.co.uk

Yes Pls
020 8600 2530

Chair covers and linens

Elite Weddings
0845 602 8851
www.eliteweddings.co.uk

Host With Style
020 8893 4823
www.hostwithstyle.co.uk

Mediterranean Occasions
www.mediterraneanoccasions.co.uk

Northfields
020 8988 7977
www.linenforhire.com

Snap Drape Hire
01568 616638
www.snapdrape.co.uk

Dress designers

Alan Hannah
www.alanhannah.co.uk

Amanda Wakeley Sposa
www.amandawakeley.com

Amanda Wyatt
01625 522344

Browns Bride
www.brownsfashion.com

Candy Anthony
www.candyanthony.com

Caroline Castigliano
www.carolinecastigliano.co.uk

Caroline Parkes
020 8871 3003

David Fielden
020 7351 0067

Ian Stuart
www.ianstuart-bride.com

Jenny Packham
www.jennypackham.com

Maggie Sottero
www.maggiesottero.com

Mirror Mirror
020 8348 2113

Pronovias
www.pronovias.com

Pronuptia
www.pronuptia.co.uk

Ritva Westenius
www.ritvawestenius.com

Stewart Parvin
020 7235 1125

Suzanne Neville
www.suzanneveville.com

Watters & Watters
www.watters.com

The Wedding Shop
020 7838 1188

Florists

British Florists Association
0870 240 3208
www.britishfloristsassocation.org

Chantal Flores Design
020 8742 9378

Flowers & Plants Association
020 7738 8044
www.flowers.org.uk

Jane Packer
020 7486 1300
www.jane-packer.co.uk

Mary Jane Vaughan
020 7385 8400
www.fastflowers.co.uk

Mathew Dickinson
020 7503 0456
www.mathewdickinsonflowers.com

Paula Pryke
020 7837 7373
www.paula-pryke-flowers.com

Wild At Heart
020 7704 6312
www.wildatheart.com

Gift List Companies

Debenhams
www.debenhams.com

Harrods
www.harrods.com

John Lewis
www.johnlewis.com

Marks & Spencer
www.marksandspencer.com

The Wedding Shop
www.weddingshop.com

Wrapit
www.wrapit.co.uk

Hen nights

Big Weekends
0870 744 2251
www.bigweekends.com

Hen Heaven
0870 770 1996
www.henheaven.co.uk

Party Bus
0845 838 5400
www.partybus.co.uk

Wicked Weekends
0870 774 0153
www.wickedweekends.co.uk

Hire companies

Jones Catering Equipment Hire
020 8320 0600
www.joneshire.co.uk

Rayners Hire
020 8870 6000
www.rayners.co.uk

Spaceworks
0800 854486
www.spaceworks.co.uk

Top Table Hire
01327 260575
www.toptablehire.com

Well Dressed Tables
www.welldressedtables.com

Honeymoons and weddings abroad

Abercrombie & Kent
0845 070 0610
www.abercrombiekent.co.uk

British Airways Holidays
0870 850 9850
www.britishairways.com

Caribtours
020 7751 0660
www.caribtours.co.uk

Carrier
www.carrier.co.uk

Elegant Resorts
01244 897222
www.elegantresorts.co.uk

First Choice
0870 850 3999
www.firstchoice.co.uk

ITC Classics
01244 355527
www.itcclassics.co.uk

Kuoni
01306 747007
www.kuoni.co.uk

Virgin Holidays
0870 990 8825
www.virginholidays.co.uk

Menswear (to hire and to buy)

Anthony Formalwear
www.anthonyformalwear.co.uk

Austin Reed
0800 585479
www.austinreed.co.uk

Debenhams
020 7408 4444
www.debenhams.co.uk

Ede & Ravenscroft
www.edandravenscroft.co.uk

Favourbrook
020 7491 2337
www.favourbrook.com

Hire Society
0870 780 2003
www.hire-society.com

Marc Wallace
020 7731 4575
www.marcwallace.com

Moss Bros Hire
020 7447 7200
www.mossbroshire.co.uk

Ozwald Boateng
www.ozwaldboateng.co.uk

Pal Zileri
020 7493 9711
www.palzileri.com

Pronuptia
01273 323046
www.pronuptia.co.uk

Young Bride & Groom
www.youngbrideandgroom.co.uk

Photography

British Institute of Professional Photography
www.bipp.com

Master Photographers Association
www.thempa.com

Society of Wedding & Portrait Photographers
www.swpp.co.uk

Speeches

MJ Consulting Speech Making Courses
01314 666051

Fine Speeches
www.finespeeches.com

Utter Wit
www.utterwit.co.uk

Wedding Speech Builder
www.weddingspeechbuilder.com

Write 4 Me
www.write4me.co.uk

Stag nights

Blokes Only
www.blokesonly.com

Extreme Activities
www.extreme-activities.com

Great Experience Days
www.greatexperiencedays.co.uk

Last Night of Freedom
www.lastnightoffreedom.co.uk

The Stag Company
www.thestagcompany.com

Stationery

Borrowed Blue Press
www.borrowedbluepress.co.uk

CCA Stationery
01772 663030
www.ccagroup.co.uk

Hello!Lucky
www.hellolucky.com

Little Cherub Design
01609 773239
www.littlecherubdesign.co.uk

Lollipop Designs
www.lollipopdesigns.co.uk

Paper Scissors
01616 787779
www.paper-scissors.com

Silver Nutmeg
01992 501464
www.silvernutmeg.com

Smythson of Bond Street
020 7629 8668
www.smythson.com

Susan O'Hanlon
01753 887659
www.stationery-wedding.com

The Wren Press
www.wrenpress.com

Toastmasters

National Association of Toastmasters
0845 838 2814
www.natuk.com

Transport

American Dreams
www.americandreams.co.uk

Antique Auto Agency
www.antique-auto-agency.co.uk

Austins
www.vintagetaxi.com

Blue Triangle Buses
www.bluetrianglebuses.com

Courtyard Carriages
www.courtyardcarriages.co.uk

Elite Helicopters
www.elitehelicopters.co.uk

Historic and Classic Car Hirers Guild
www.hchg.co.uk

Karma Kabs
www.karmakabs.com

The Marriage Carriage Company
www.themarriagecarriagecompany.co.uk

Memory Lane
www.memorylane.co.uk

Starlite Limos
www.starlitelimos.co.uk

Wedding planners

Alison Price
020 7840 7640
www.alisonprice.co.uk

Carole Sobell
020 8200 8111
ww.carolesobell.com

Deborah Dwek
020 8446 9501
www.deborahdwekweddings.co.uk

Idyllic Days
www.idyllicdays.com

Kathryn Lloyd
020 7828 5535
www.kathrynlloyd.co.uk

Supreme Events
020 7499 3345
www.supremeevents.co.uk

Wedding Bible Events
01235 538126
www.weddingbible.co.uk

Wedding shows

The Designer Wedding Show
www.designerweddingshow.co.uk

The National Wedding Show
www.nationalweddingshow.co.uk

The UK Wedding Shows
www.theukweddingshows.co.uk

The Wedding Planner Index

Page numbers in **bold** indicate major references